Daphne Jackson was born in Westmorland in 1907 and trained as a journalist before moving to Java with her husband in the late 1920s, to work for a Java plantation company. She and her husband were interned separately by the Japanese upon their arrival in 1942. Daphne Jackson has three children, two of whom were born in Java, and now lives in St Austell, Cornwall.

DAPHNE JACKSON

Java Nightmare

GRAFTON BOOKS

A Division of the Collins Publishing Group

LONDON GLASGOW
TORONTO SYDNEY AUCKLAND

Grafton Books
A Division of the Collins Publishing Group
8 Grafton Street, London W1X 3LA

Published by Grafton Books 1989

First published in Great Britain by
Tabb House, Church Street, Padstow, Cornwall, 1979

Copyright © Daphne Jackson 1979

ISBN 0-586-20367-2

Printed and bound in Great Britain by
Collins, Glasgow

Set in Melior

To Ferne, in memory of her mother

Foreword

by Harold L. Payne OBE
President of the National Federation of Far Eastern
POW Clubs and Associations

I deem it a great privilege to have the opportunity to write the Foreword to this enthralling book. Much has been written about the male side of captivity under the Japanese during the period 1942 to 1945. *Java Nightmare* fulfils a need, in being a factual history of a woman who suffered the unfortunate experience of being interned by the Japanese in Java.

This book relates the vivid story of life in various women's camps, commencing with the early days of internment when families had been segregated into male and female camps. There were women of many different nationalities herded together learning to live a communal life, with no privacy and under great duress.

As the story unfolds it tells of the different hardships these women had to endure at the hands of their captors. In doing so, the author shows how human frailty comes to grips with life when tested to the utmost of its endurance. Furthermore the book leaves no doubt in the reader's mind that when faced with a situation such as these women were – living on a starvation diet with little or no medicine and no contact with the outside world – out of this horror can grow some of the strongest and most enduring bonds of friendship.

The author also on the other hand gives instances of internees who sadly weakened under the strain, acting in very unsocial ways; fortunately such persons were in a minority.

When at last the war ended and their captivity was over, life did not become easy overnight, as was anticipated, and the book clearly outlines the problems which they had to face on being released.

This is a wonderful true story of great courage in the face of great adversity.

Contents

Contents

Java Nightmare

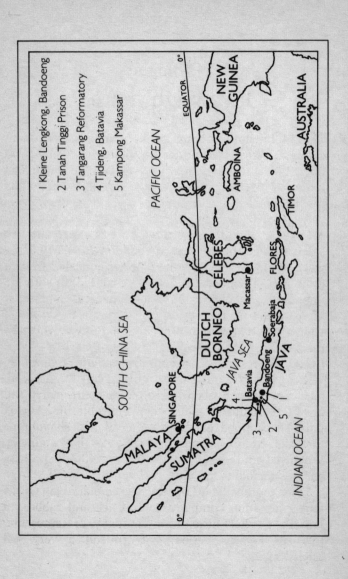

1 Kleine Lengkong, Bandoeng
2 Tanah Tinggi Prison
3 Tangarang Reformatory
4 Tjideng, Batavia
5 Kampong Makassar

Prologue

This is the story of some of the women's internment camps in West Java under the Japanese. There were many others throughout what was then the Dutch East Indies, as elsewhere in Asia, but I can only write of the five in which I was myself interned over three years between 1942 and 1945.

In 1927, when I had been working as a secretary to a small metal brokers' firm in London for £3.10.0 per week, living in a residential club for educated women (now part of London University), I got fed up with the long hours on poor pay, and the general depression then starting in the country. One day a friend and I visited a well-known fortune teller in Putney, who gave me brief, but quite accurate, details of my life – I was twenty at the time – then told me that within months I would get a job out East through a tall Englishman, meet my future husband on a tennis court, marry and have three children and a very enjoyable life. At that point she stopped, and after a long silence, she told me that she could see nothing more for black clouds. Whether I got through that period to further happiness she was unable to tell me.

Three months later I obtained a secretarial job with a large plantation company, mainly tea and rubber, in Java: the Far East head of the Company, or Representative as he was called, was indeed a very tall Englishman.

Charles Jackson, the Rubber Superintendent, who was on leave when I arrived in March, 1929, returned in the autumn, and by July the following year I was allowed to break my contract so we could be married in Soebang in the Big House, the beautiful but enormous bungalow used by the head of the firm. We later had three daughters, the youngest of whom died within months of her birth of a sudden fever.

Every third year we had summer leave in England, and in 1937 we left our eldest daughter Daphne at home to continue her education, intending to return home for good the following leave to run a small farm we had bought, with sitting tenants, in South Cornwall. Jane, then four, returned with us to Java.

As the war in the Far East exploded, my husband was able to get permission for some of the younger Britishers to leave and join up in India, despite heavy pressure on the Company to make all-out efforts to get away as much rubber, tea, quinine and other products as possible.

Then, following the loss of his son in the RAF over Egypt, Mr Adams, the head of the Company, had to return to England to his wife, who was seriously ill, and my husband was ordered by phone from London to take over as Representative.

Early in 1942 Lord Wavell and his staff had come to stay in a hotel in Lembang, a hill station above Bandoeng in West Java. Charles was involved in housing soldiers and other members of the British Forces in temporary huts in the rubber gardens until they could be got away to safety. Secret meetings also took place in the Directors' beautiful house at Tengeragoeng in the hills above Soebang where the Admiral and General in charge of Dutch Forces met with the British to discuss the urgent situation. One day members of the World's Press, including Edward Ward, H. R. Knickerbocker and others, suddenly appeared in Soebang to interview Charles.

My husband did all he could to help both Dutch and British in any way possible, and because of this was later to be taken by the Japanese Secret Police for interrogation. When 84 Squadron of the RAF arrived from Singapore by way of Sumatra in Java, my husband was contacted. Though the bombers were to be added to those being used on the nearby Dutch military aerodrome at Kalidjati, there was no room for the men. Some two hundred and fifty RAF were looked after, either in the Big House or in two other large bungalows in Soebang, until the arrival of the Japanese and the hasty evacuation to the hills.

At the same time preparations were being made by the Dutch to defend the eight thousand islands, some enormous, of what had been for three and a half centuries a priceless possession, namely, the Dutch East Indies. Originally captured for the immense wealth to be obtained from the Spice Islands, in more recent years there had been rumblings of mutiny and calls for independence by natives of the islands. When I arrived in Java in 1928 there were incipient mutinies in the Army, and parts of the archipelago had uprisings.

In Java itself, one of the few islands into which wealth had been returned in the form of agriculture, education and commerce, there were two distinct languages: high and low Soendanese in West Java, and high and low Javanese in mid- and East Java, and the same applied in Sumatra, Borneo and New Guinea. For the sake of clarity I shall refer to all such peoples as Indonesian, as they later became. I shall use Batavia, the Dutch name for the capital city of Java, though it has now reverted to the old name of Djakarta.

My own servants, when they later, with great courage, came to see me in Tjioemboeloeit, the Bandoeng suburb where I lived until internment, told me they were going to fight. I took this to mean for the Dutch, but later understood that the Japanese invasion was going to be used by large numbers of Indonesians to regain their thousand years' inheritance, and form a new republic.

1

Soebang – the Japanese Invasion

Soebang, the Company headquarters where we lived, was about one hundred miles from Batavia (now Djakarta), and forty from Bandoeng, our nearest large hill town. The Company estates, about twenty of them, ran from the sea on the north coast of Java up to the sides of an extinct volcano of six thousand feet, the whole block forming an area of land about the size of Kent. The road to Bandoeng led through a pass beneath the wooded slopes of the crater past Lembang, and down into the plain of Garoet.

With the Japanese army already fighting its way down through Malaya, many British and American women – the latter by order of their Consulate – left Java to get to Australia or India. At the same time refugees were fleeing from Singapore and Malaya to what was then the Dutch East Indies, now the Republic of Indonesia.

No Dutch families were supposed to leave the Indies, by order of the Government, and it was obvious that in the event of a Japanese invasion, the masses of women and children would be a very big problem.

It is always easy to be wise after the event, but it would certainly have been better if all who wished to leave had been allowed to do so in good time. Instead, many ships went away empty in January 1942, and more were uselessly scuttled at the last moment both in Batavia and Soerabaja.

By January, the Japanese had fought their way down through Burma and Malaya, and the fall of Singapore was imminent. In Java, belated preparations to meet an invasion were being made. The estate managers were asked to push all production as fast as possible, whilst in their limited spare time they trained for Home Guard duties.

Charles had originally hoped to get away himself, as he was still on the reserve of his old Indian regiment, the 37th Dogras, but after becoming Representative, he and the remaining Britishers were attached to the Soebang Defence Corps.

In January, at a weekly meeting of group leaders of our Company organization, I explained that both my husband and I felt it would be wiser if the women with children were moved to some safer place in the hills. In this way, a communal centre could be started at once, and lessen the danger of evacuation at the last moment.

There was immediately great opposition, partly because many Dutchwomen believed implicitly that their Government would look after them, and partly because a Regulation had just been issued stating that if children from estates or elsewhere were brought into Bandoeng or Batavia, they would not be accepted in the schools there. This to the Dutch was a very real threat, for a child who did not pass his exams well enough to move from class to class each year, and so gain his final diploma, had little chance of getting a job.

It was useless to argue that a child was better alive, even without his school diploma, so the meeting broke up.

The following day, several of the mothers came to tell me that they had been to see the *Controleur* – the only Dutch Government official at our Company headquarters – and he had advised them to stay where they were, saying they would be looked after by their Government, and in the event of invasion, evacuated by the Army.

The women were quite adamant in their refusal to move, so the organization which had been built up with so much labour lapsed.

When the Big House (the enormous historic bungalow in which we lived) had been made ready for possible evacuees from the estates, the windows of the large bedrooms were wired against mosquitoes, and twenty hessian beds on steel frames put in each of the three largest rooms. The whole L-shaped building, the frontage of which measured some two hundred feet, was blacked out with hundreds of metres of cloth, so that the rooms inside could be fully lighted.

After the breakup of the women's organization, I felt that these, and many other preparations, had been wasted. But one morning, 15 February 1942, my husband called me out of a Red Cross meeting to say Singapore had fallen. He asked if I could make arrangements to take a large number of RAF from 84 Squadron. They had escaped by way of Sumatra, and though the bombers would be stationed at the Dutch Air Force aerodrome at Kalidjati, about ten miles away, there was not sufficient accommodation for all the RAF and some were to be quartered in Soebang.

The preparations already made for the women were now of use, for, besides the Big House, two other bungalows had been partially cleared of furniture.

Putting a Dutch and a British woman in charge of each house, we immediately had three messes ready. As Charles and I were only using the separate pavilion suite of rooms, we were able to house seventy-five men in the rest of our palatial bungalow.

At that time, though our youngest daughter Jane was still in Java, she was living in the hill house with Miss Andrews, an elderly missionary who had escaped from Sarawak and come to us to teach Jane.

Despite the continual air raid warnings, Jane had been amazingly good. I had made her a siren suit with a little forage cap, and she joined the Indonesian squad who had their quarters in our garden during the day and, when there was an alarm, she was allowed to bang on the big wooden drum. That duty carried out, Jane, then nine, used to squat on the verandah, or under the billiard-table, and tell the Indonesians fairy stories in Malay, much to their enjoyment. Luckily there never was any bombing in Soebang itself, and before 84 Squadron arrived, Jane was in the hill house.

When the RAF did arrive in the blackout one night, they were amazed, after the terrible time they had been through in Singapore, to find the house fully lit inside, and apparently a normal life going on. Many of them were resentful that they had been ordered out of yet another country, and were still very much under the influence of the dreadful scenes they had witnessed before Singapore fell.

However, after two or three days' rest, things got sorted out, and with the help of Bob Paxton, an Australian who became liaison officer, meals were served fairly regularly.

At first we met many of the men, and I got to know

them when serving meals, but after a short while, as place after place became vacant at supper, and it always seemed to be the lad who had asked me to have his best girl's photo reframed, or his shoes mended, who was killed, I felt if I was to do my job properly, it was better I knew no one by name.

With the help of our house servants, about ten of them, who did wonderful work, we served breakfasts and suppers to anything up to seventy men, and lunches and teas to a few. Teas were not on the rations menu, but there were always a few men who got back to rush the bathrooms, which had the luxury of hot water laid on, and to try some of the Chinese cook's best cake.

Although it was not supposed to be known that British airmen were housed in Soebang, each time a Japanese plane came over, out they rushed, determined to have a bang with their rifles. On one occasion, when nearly all the Company men were out on 'manoeuvres', there was a parachute warning. Immediately those RAF off duty tore out, intent on searching the rubber gardens for the Japanese. Luckily they were stopped before they got far, for most of them had not the faintest idea of the difference between a Japanese and an Indonesian, and might have got into a lot of trouble, particularly as the alarm turned out to be false.

On Friday 27 October, the British Consul rang my husband from Batavia, and Charles then decided to evacuate the British women and children on his own initiative. I went to the nearby bungalows to warn the women to be ready to leave at an hour's notice, with one suitcase each.

We had made arrangements that in the event of evacuation our daughter was to travel with Nell Miller, who would be leaving with her husband, as he was getting on in years. Jane came down from the hills with Miss Andrews, who unfortunately refused to leave, and in the afternoon my husband sent all the British women and children, with the exception of Miss Andrews, a Dutch girl married to a Scotsman, and myself, under convoy to Tjilatjap, a port on the south coast of Java where they were to try to get a ship.

They travelled with a senior member of staff in convoy, and after a bad journey reached Tjilatjap, where they had to wait twenty-four hours before embarking. Very luckily so, as it turned out. Four years later we learned that they finally sailed on the *Zaandam*, which went direct to Fremantle, Western Australia, without dropping the pilot. The other ships which went out before her were blown up as they left harbour, including one with 750 women and children on board.

At this time heavy fighting was going on in the Java Sea, when several ships were lost, including the flagship, *De Ruyter*, the *Java*, and later the *Houston* and *Perth*.

On the last day of February, 1942, rumours began to circulate Soebang that Java was practically without protection from the sea or air. In view of this, my husband was amazed to hear that the Home Guard had been given several hours off-duty. This was quite inexplicable to us, and even more so to the RAF officers and men who were stationed with us, who had some idea of the critical situation.

At night members of the staff even met in the Club for a film, and when I told one woman that I thought

—

things were very serious, she said in Dutch, 'I don't see a cloud in the sky.'

Shortly afterwards, about ten o'clock, my husband was called to the telephone at the same time as Mr Houwing, manager of Soebang rubber estate and head of the Dutch Home Guard. The news they heard was bad. A convoy of Japanese transports was approaching the Company's port of Pamanoekan on the north coast. Despite bombing by the remains of the Dutch and British Air Forces for thirty-six hours at a stretch, the situation looked extremely unpleasant.

We left the Club, and returned to the Big House, where my husband changed into a khaki suit and went to join his brigade at the Company workshops. He told me coffee and sandwiches were needed at Kalidjati urgently, and the truck which collected them shortly afterwards brought four or five of 84 Squadron, who were absolutely dead beat. Apart from these men and Macdonald, who had taken over as liaison on his arrival from Malaya, where he had been a police officer, there were only Miss Andrews, one or two servants and myself in the house.

I warned her what was happening, and then went and sat by the telephone, though even then I had really no idea how serious the situation was.

At midnight one of the Dutch staff, now a sergeant-major in the Home Guard, rang me and told me to pack a bag and be ready to leave at short notice. I went to tell Miss Andrews that she would only be able to take one case.

As I fully expected we should have to trudge up the hill road over the pass to Bandoeng, I decided I would put a couple of changes of clothing, together with photos of the family and my passport, in a blanket, as this would be easy to carry. It seemed ridiculous, even dangerous, to take jewels, and in fact I picked up the most trivial things as I wandered from room to room. I put a few oddments in a tiny blue leather case, and then went and sat on the deserted verandah. I had warned Mac, but he decided to let his men sleep for the present.

After a while Miss Andrews joined me. It was a brilliant moonlight night, and perfectly peaceful, except when the wooden shutters on the windows rattled from time to time with the firing of guns somewhere in the distance. The telephone rang again, shrilling loudly in the still night, and when I answered it, I was told to leave Soebang immediately. I explained to the Dutch officer speaking that the cars which had taken the British women and children to Tjilatjap had not returned, and I was therefore without transport. After some conversation at the other end of the phone, I was told someone with a car would take Miss Andrews and me to the Club, where we should be able to get transport to the hill estate at which all the Dutch women and children were assembling.

At 4 A.M. the lieutenant arrived with a two-seater, and Mac helped us in with our luggage. He asked how long it would be before the Japanese came. 'Three hours,' replied the lieutenant, and I went cold down my spine.

He left us on the big open verandah of the Club, where only six hours previously we had been peacefully watching a film. For the next fifteen minutes we watched helplessly as car after car rushed up the hill towards Bandoeng and safety.

I signalled frantically with a torch, and at last Mrs Wansink, the doctor's wife, stopped her already heavily loaded car. She was able to take Miss Andrews, and also the young wife of one of the staff who had joined us moments before in a highly nervous state.

The next twenty minutes or so I waited alone on the empty verandah of the huge Club, and I have never been so frightened in my life. The moonlight played all sorts of tricks, and every moment I expected a Japanese to jump over the low balustrade.

Instead, a stream of women and children began to arrive. After that I was too busy trying to get transport to have time to think of Japanese. Women and children, some on foot and some on bicycles, some dragging dogs, and all with luggage of various shapes and sizes, staggered up the drive in the early morning light. I smashed a door and got in to the Club telephone, to try frantically to arrange for cars, lorries or any form of transport to get the people away in time.

As fast as some families were sent off, more arrived. But just as things seemed quite hopeless, three men arrived from Soekamandi, our sisal and tapioca estate by the sea, driving their own cars. Strictly against Government orders, my husband had evacuated all the women and children from this estate to the hills some time previously, and though he had been ordered to fetch them back, fortunately he had not done so. Now the men agreed to take some families to the meeting place in the hills before going on to join their families in Bandoeng.

Soon more cars came, some driven by Europeans and some by native chauffeurs, and gradually most of the women and children got away.

A Dutch soldier came up on his motorbike and told us that everyone had been warned to leave. It was quite impossible to check who had gone and who not, and I dared not return to the Big House for my old evacuation list in case some women left the Club and returned home, feeling that would be safer.

To my horror, the Dutch nursing sister from our Company hospital came and told me she still had eight British wounded there, as well as Company patients, and that she did not intend to leave.

Sister Jansen was a very brave woman, and returned to the hospital with the apothecary and his wife. I promised that if I could get cars for the women still waiting, and someone to attend to them – two of the last arrivals were expecting babies, and insisted on travelling together with their other children – I would join her.

Whilst we waited for more transport, we distractedly tore up maps, the tears meanwhile rolling down our cheeks. We were tired and overwrought, and had no news of our husbands, or in some cases of our families, and every now and then I caught the sarcastic laughter of two women and a man who had seated themselves on the verandah to watch the fun. They were members of the National Socialist Bond – Dutch Fascists – and were staying in Soebang to meet the Japanese.

After a time Mrs Esveld arrived, who had formerly been a nurse, and she later travelled with the expectant mothers. Then Mr Houwing rushed in, horrified to find any of us still at the Club, for the Japanese were expected at any moment.

He ordered us to leave. I regret to this day that I did not manage to get a message to Mac, so that he might have had a chance to collect the men from the hospital in a truck, however ill they were, and get them and the nurse away.

If the Kalidjati hospital had not been full, they would never have been in the Company one, but it should have been one of the Army's first jobs to get the wounded away.

Mr Houwing is dead. He died in prison of a broken heart. He was a dear, kind man who undoubtedly did his best in very difficult circumstances, but that no one should have thought of the hospital, or made some attempt to remove the patients, seems to me quite unbearable, especially in view of what followed.

2

The Bandoeng Refugees

Although the Commandant, Mr Houwing, ordered us to leave at once, it looked as though we should have to walk up the long road to the hills, for no transport was available.

At the last moment two cars driven by native chauffeurs did appear, and the last of the evacuees including the two expectant mothers and their children were bundled in. As we turned out of the Club drive, the chauffeur in my car lost his nerve and pulled up, saying he did not know the road. Luckily the works *mandoer*, the Indonesian head of all the Company's chauffeurs, was standing beside the road. He jumped on the running-board, changed places with the chauffeur, and drove off at top speed up the hill. Within minutes the Japanese had entered Soebang, where they were to stay for the next three and a half years.

On reaching the first hill estate to which we had been ordered we found only Mrs Houwing and her dog, and were told to drive on to a higher tea estate, taking the dog with us. I found later that many of the Dutch women had been warned early the previous evening, and had left – in some cases in a car to themselves – and taken a great deal of luggage and also their dogs.

When we eventually reached Boekanegara, the highest tea and quinine estate, some of the hill managers' wives had provided a meal of rice. All the women and children had at least floor space, and were given very welcome food.

I spoke to Mrs Houwing, who had now arrived after having had a telephone conversation with her husband, and I gathered that all our men had now left Soebang after terrible fighting, and were moving behind us up the hill. This later proved to be untrue, but at the time it added to our worries. I was most anxious about Jane and the British families, of whom we had heard nothing, as well as my husband.

It also seemed to me that the Dutch women and children should not stay on at Boekanegara, as my husband had warned me if ever we had to evacuate we must not stop at that estate if we could help it. Boekanegara was just below the big fortifications on the road over the pass to Bandoeng, and so likely to prove a very unhealthy spot. I explained this to Mrs Houwing, but she said she had her orders. There was nothing further I could do.

Another worry was the three men from Soekamandi who had brought women and children to Boekanegara. Not unnaturally, after depositing them safely, they had hurried on over the pass to find their wives and children. If we did have to leave the estate, we were going to find ourselves appallingly short of transport.

It was the time of the monsoon. Women gathered in frightened groups, huddled for warmth in coats and scarves against the rain. Little children kept close, but the older ones fought and argued and got under everyone's feet. The scene made me think of the refugees arriving in a ship off the United States in some painting I'd seen.

Just as everyone was trying to get some rest, a phone

call came through, and we had orders to leave immediately and proceed to Bandoeng, as the one bridge had to be blown up behind us. After some panic, everyone piled into the remaining cars – thirty-nine women and children had come up from Soebang, and about twenty-five more joined us in the hills – and we set off.

The road from the estate was thick mud after the heavy rain, and once again the *mandoer* was to prove invaluable. Taking over the wheel, he drove car after car up the worst slippery slopes to the top. When we finally got over the pass on the main Bandoeng road, our convoy had to wait for some time for Dutch troops moving up to man the fortifications: Soebang, only about twenty miles down the other side of the mountain, had then been in Japanese hands for some hours.

At Lembang, a hill village where till recently Lord Wavell and his staff had been quartered, we were told to leave the cars and go into a transit camp.

After much argument, we were finally allowed to proceed to Bandoeng, which was apparently already crammed with people from all the surrounding estates. I arranged that such women as could not get accommodation with friends should join me at the Homann Hotel, in the centre of the town, where I would do my best to help them.

Eventually six of us shared a room. Air raid alarms were frequent, and the town was packed with British and Dutch soldiers, and refugees from Malaya, Sumatra and the other Indonesian islands.

When we had been ordered away from Boekanegara, some of the wives had so much luggage that it was necessary to stow it in an unused ambulance, which was to follow behind the convoy of cars – I only learned of this later. The first days in Bandoeng, when we still had no idea whether our husbands were alive or dead, the telephone rang constantly in our room, and I was asked by irate women whether I knew the ambulance had gone over a ravine and all the luggage was lost. Would the Company be responsible for the insurance?

On Monday 2 March 1942, I went with some of the Company wives to the Municipal Offices, to try to get permits for us all to stop in Bandoeng. The whole compound outside was a milling mass of gesticulating, angry women. The noise was appalling. Eventually I got inside and filled in the appropriate forms, only to be very rudely received by a young Dutch official when I told him I would be responsible for the women until my husband arrived.

Later that evening this man came to the hotel to apologize for his brusqueness, saying he had been so amazed to find anyone who would take responsibility at that moment that he could not believe his ears! He promised if I would let him have a list of the names of the women and children concerned, he would give me a permit. Further trouble came when he did not receive my list, as the messenger either could not, or did not, deliver it, but at last I got a copy along and all was well.

On the Tuesday afternoon Corrie Meyer, the wife of one of the office staff now a sergeant-major in the Home Guard, was in our room with me when there was a violent knocking on the door. In rushed a wild, unshaven Dutch soldier, with a rifle in his hand, asking for his wife. I did not recognize him, but fortunately Corrie did. Mr Buyteweg had left the Company to do his military service, and before leaving had had his

wife and children moved from their estate house near
Kalidjati aerodrome to a bungalow on a tea estate,
which was less likely to be bombed.

On the morning of the evacuation she should have
been warned by the manager of the estate but had not
been, and as I knew nothing of her whereabouts I was
very upset. Rather hopelessly I sent Mr Buyteweg to
the Dutch Assistant Resident of Bandoeng, though he
had been far from helpful in finding accommodation
for the Company wives. At about five o'clock the two
of them came back to the hotel.

By this time Buyteweg was nearly frantic for he had
discovered that his wife had never left the hill estate,
and nobody knew how far up the hillside the Japanese
had already come. All the Assistant Resident could do
was to tell him to keep calm, so Buyteweg took matters
into his own hands and decided to make his way over
the pass to rescue his family, if they were still alive.

Mr Colijn, a journalist, volunteered to go with him,
and they were given an escort when they reached the
top of the pass. They found Mrs Buyteweg and the
children alive and well, though they had been through
a terrible experience, and brought them safely back to
Bandoeng the next morning.

On Tuesday night Corrie heard that her husband and
the other Soebang men had walked over the hill and
got as far as Lembang. He and the Dutch officers arrived
in Bandoeng late that night. The following morning the
Britishers and the Dutch soldiers limped in, and
Charles proceeded to get the British demobilized at
once, so that those who wished could join up with the
British forces then in Java. He also saw Dr van Mook,
the Lieutenant-Governor General, who was under

orders from the Dutch Government to leave Java immediately. He told my husband to get away as many people as possible.

After finding a room in a pension for Miss Andrews, who, together with another British woman, decided to try to leave from the South Coast and then changed her mind again, my husband and I, together with some of the British staff, set up an office in a building belonging to our Bandoeng agents.

The Japanese landings in three places in Java – one of them Pamanoekan – had been so rapid and successful that the whole island was in the most chaotic state. Families were cut off from one another, and many of the wives of staff away in the Dutch Army came to the office in the hope of getting some reliable information. Though there had been practically no fighting for Bandoeng itself, several men had been shot whilst leaving our estates, and some of the staff had been killed by Japanese whom they unexpectedly met on the outskirts of the village.

Mr Levert, who went back, against orders, to rescue a large sum of Company money which had been cached in a secret place, was murdered by the native troops with him, and thrown down a well. A Lowlands manager was caught and shot by looters when he returned to his estate to retrieve a case for his wife. A third manager, Mr Marin, was knifed by natives when he was caught on his estate, brought into Soebang tied to a pole, and reputedly buried alive, though we heard later that he was dead when he was brought in.

Several other staff members came into contact with the Japanese most unexpectedly, when they were travelling in three freight cars of Indonesian troops from Soekamandi to Soebang on the Sunday morning. Most of the men escaped, but one was shot, and two other Europeans escaped to Bandoeng, after hiding underneath native huts and in the jungle for several days. One man had a bullet in him, but nevertheless managed to escape successfully, and what is more, the European who escaped with him arrived safely at the office still holding the bag with the estate cash!

One of the first people to come to the office was Mrs Buyteweg, the wife who had been left behind in the hills, and I was thankful to see her safe and well. She brought cheese and butter, knowing we were by that time living in the office. I thought it most generous of her after the terrible time she had experienced.

The Indonesians had apparently come to her bungalow, and told her to dress in a *sarong* and bring the children to the *kampong* (native village). They made it clear that had it not been for the children, they would have killed her.

Reports now began to come through by escaping Indonesians and others of what had happened in Soebang when the Europeans left. Within a few moments, a mad gang of about three hundred men, women and children had started looting the Big House and other bungalows, burning, smashing and stealing. This did not seem to me surprising, since they must have been very frightened when the Europeans walked out on them.

The nurse, Sister Jansen, and the apothecary had revolvers at the hospital, and they hurriedly tried to hide the British patients when all the shouting started, as they expected the Indonesians to come to the hospital also.

Instead, it was the Japanese who came, and so they were caught, in Red Cross uniform, with revolvers, and taken prisoner, as were the patients. Many other refugees, including a Dutch woman and a little fair-haired girl, a Dutch dominie, and many soldiers were caught in Soebang, and after ten days all of them were bayoneted into open trenches. After the war these trenches were found to contain over three hundred bodies.

Many conflicting reports were in circulation about the state of the fighting in Java, but at the end of the week the Dutch capitulated.

On Monday 9 March, all guests at the Hotel Hamann where we had been staying were told to get out. The Japanese Storm Troopers were taking over.

My husband and I, together with six or seven Britishers and a sack of rice, went to a bungalow owned by a doctor just on the outskirts of Bandoeng, where we heard we could get accommodation if we brought our own food. It had been a sanatorium previously, and some of us were given beds in tiny cells along a verandah, which had been used for patients. The beds were still warm.

While we were sitting on a verandah, waiting for some rice to be cooked for our evening meal, a bullet came whizzing through the trees to our right, then further shots. Some of the men went down the drive to see what had happened, and found a wounded native lying on the road. He and his friend had been standing watching a group of Storm Troopers go into a house, and when the Japanese shouted to them, they of course

could not understand. The next thing they knew, one
had a bullet in his ribs.

This was our first introduction to the occupying
troops, and the incident depressed us. After a miserable
meal of half-cooked rice, and a bit of chocolate, we sat
in the blackout trying to get the BBC on the wireless,
and then turned in.

Early next morning, when I was dressed and Charles
shaving, the shuttered window was rudely opened, and
some Japanese soldiers came in. They grunted and
shuffled, and looked at various things. One of them
signed he wanted my husband's watch, in exchange for
one he had. I begged Charles to do as the man asked,
and the soldiers went off down the passage. It turned
out later that the watch belonged to the doctor, to
whom Charles returned it.

Next, we were all called to the front of the bungalow,
and told to leave at once. We had come by car, and
expected it to be commandeered, but except for a
banging on the behind with the flat of a bayonet, we
were allowed to leave without further trouble, the men
with their knapsacks containing their remaining possessions, and I with my blanket bundle.

We drove back to Bandoeng wondering what to do,
and eventually decided to try to reach the agent's office,
and use that temporarily. Just before we got there, the
car was commandeered by the Japanese, but we were
left unmolested, and walked the short remaining distance to our new home.

The office was glass-fronted, though fortunately the
lower part had been boarded up because of the bombing, and we settled in the front room. Next door was a
Chinese restaurant, where we could still get a meal, but

the Japanese declared a six o'clock curfew, so in the evening, with the eight Britishers who had by then joined us, we locked the office doors and settled down to pass a very unpleasant time.

The whole night Japanese Storm Troopers, freight cars and army equipment moved along the street, which was a main one in the centre of Bandoeng, while Japanese guards shuffled round the buildings, making sleep impossible. Every moment I waited for a bang on the door.

When daylight came, we were heartily thankful. We were then able to go out to the washroom at the back of the office, and try to freshen up a bit.

Our agents imported, amongst other things, Spratts Dog Biscuits, and these, plus a tin of jam which Lofty Masefield still had, made a slightly unorthodox breakfast.

During the days that followed, we were helped again and again by one of the Company's staff who had escaped to Bandoeng. Mr Spit had only been taken temporarily onto the staff, and he was not young, but when possible he braved the curfew and risked being shot to bring us food. When the Britishers were interned, he continued to look after me and help me in every way possible. Sadly, he later died in camp.

Another man who helped us, at the risk of execution, was the Chinese owner of the restaurant, who then, and later, got food to us each night.

By the end of the week, those staff who had gone to join the British troops somewhere in West Java came back again, as the 'Cease-fire' had been given. The office became more and more congested, so we took

over additional rooms, and by Sunday night there were
nineteen men and myself in the building.

By day we still worked with the Red Cross and tried
to keep contact with the Company's staff. One day a
Red Cross man came in, and said he had been over the
mountain nearly to Soebang. On the way back, he had
called in at a bungalow, and found a Bible, with the
photo of a small girl inside, which he hoped to return
to the owner. When he showed it to me, I saw it was a
photo of Daphne, our elder daughter, which I had given
to an Australian friend. I had little thought to see it
again in such sad circumstances.

From time to time the Japanese came to the office to
talk to my husband, and the first time one shuffled in I
smiled rather nervously, and was promptly shouted at
for my insolence. After that I was careful to keep my
features rigid, in case by doing something wrong one
of the Britishers would resent the tone of the Japanese,
and get into trouble through me.

At night Charles and I had a small room to ourselves,
and I managed to get a square of mosquito net from
somewhere, which I fixed with drawing pins to the
wall over my head, for the mosquitoes were ferocious.
We slept on the floor, using large tomes from the
bookcase for pillows – mine was a large volume on the
laying of cement, which seemed eminently suitable.

All night long there was shouting and the sound of
firing from the street, and once, when the men were
playing some card game, there was a knock on the door
and two Japanese walked in. Apparently they found
nothing strange in so many people living in one office,
and went out again. We all breathed a sigh of relief,

particularly as each evening we tried to get some news on an aged wireless.

When the British women and children left for Tjilatjap, we were not told their destination, and no one had returned with news. One night I did hear that *Zaandam* had arrived safely in Fremantle, but at the time the news conveyed nothing to me.

One afternoon Charles and I walked up to the hospital where many British wounded were being looked after, to try to see Mr Crichton, a Consulate man who had remained behind. He had no news for us, and indeed the whole situation looked very black. As we walked back towards the centre of the town, it started to pour with rain. Just as we were trying hopefully to get a native pony cart, a large car drove past. It was the Company Cadillac, and inside were two Japanese. This was one of the cars taken by the Japanese on the way back from Tjilatjap, and as we stood soaked to the skin we heartily loathed every Japanese in sight.

Life in the Bandoeng office became daily more difficult, not only because we were living through a very anxious time, but also because we were feeling the strain of uncertainty as to what might happen to us. Almost hourly my husband was besieged by anxious men and women who had escaped from Batavia and Semarang, as well as Soebang and the estates. All sought news or help of some kind, which he always found time to give. He was an example to us all, and a great help to everyone with his patient kindness and courage.

After some weeks of this unpleasant existence, we were lent a bungalow below Tjioemboeloeit, a residential suburb, and seven of us moved there for the weekend. Not only had Charles and I a room of our own with wash-basin and beds in it, but each morning we woke to brilliant sunshine, and a really breathtaking view of the plain of Garoet which lay spread out below us.

Unfortunately this happiness was very brief. The owner of the bungalow, a Belgian woman whose husband was in the Dutch Diplomatic Service in Japan, was afraid her husband might get into trouble if it was found that the house had been lent to the British – he was in hospital at the time. On the Monday morning she told us tearfully that we must go.

Back we went, to the floor of the office and all the horrible noises in the night. Luckily, my husband heard there was another empty house higher up in the same suburb. It belonged to a Dutch engineer with whom he had once travelled and he hastily rang the owner and asked if we might rent it. Gerrit van Galen Last, who later became a great friend and, with his wife Ita, gave me endless help, immediately told us to go ahead and use the house, together with a smaller bungalow which lay alongside. Some of the men went up at once, and when the office shut, we walked up the hill to join them.

The large house was a two-storey one containing a parquet-floored lounge and dining room, a big study, cloakroom, pantries and servants' quarters on the ground floor. Upstairs were three bedrooms, two with verandahs, and bathrooms.

The smaller bungalow had a long lounge dining room, three bedrooms and a bathroom, besides a modern kitchen and servants' quarters, washroom, etc. The houses stood in small gardens, each with separate garage and drive, the bungalow lying considerably lower than the house. All around were other pleasant houses in lovely gardens, and there was a magnificent view over the plain in which Bandoeng lay. After being shut in the office in the middle of the town, it was like paradise.

There was very little furniture in either house or bungalow, as both had been used temporarily by some of the British Navy as offices before they were evacuated. The floor in the house was badly stained, giving the impression that the previous occupants had spent the time flinging bottles of ink at one another, but maybe this was done when the Japanese Storm Troopers entered Bandoeng.

Such was our new home, and we were simply delighted with it. Charles and I and three men took possession of the bungalow, whilst the remaining nine men stayed in the house, where we all met for meals. During the day three of us walked down the hill and worked in the office, and two men took turns daily as cooks, whilst the others did the cleaning, fetching food, and so on. Our numbers varied at different times, as other men came and went. Three RAF officers (one was Mac who had been with us in Soebang) arrived, having left their camp in Garoet and brought a car via Bandoeng en route for Buitenzorg, as they had heard that the POW camp there was much better! Everything was still chaotic, but it took some pluck to leave a camp under the eyes of the Japanese, who must have wondered what on earth was happening.

Mac and his companions spent a night with us, and the following morning gave us a lift into Bandoeng, which was a pleasant change from our usual hour's walk.

They had no passes of any sort, but nobody stopped us, and we arrived safely at the office. From there the RAF men calmly went out and did some shopping in the Bragaweg, the main European shopping quarter, and then, after a final beer with us, went merrily on their way.

3

Charles is Taken Away

Towards the end of March all British and American civilians were ordered to register their names, and after some debate we did this, giving our address in the suburb of Tjioemboeloeit where we were living.

We still had two of the Company's cars in the garages, but were unable to use them as we had neither passes nor petrol, though no doubt we could have obtained the latter if we could have managed the passes which were very strictly controlled by the Japanese.

On the evening of 15 April we had finished our simple supper, and while some of the men were trying to get Perth, Western Australia, on the radio, four of us were playing bridge. My husband was reading nearby, and everything was quiet and peaceful.

Suddenly, without any warning, though one or two of the men were sitting out on the terrace, there was a knock on the front door, and a party of Japanese officers and some soldiers came in with a part-Japanese interpreter.

We were ordered to stay where we were, and after some talk my husband was told that he must go for further questioning. The Japanese were perfectly polite, and eventually a few of them left with my husband and three other men, and drove off in a private car.

The interpreter said that they would all be back shortly, and that we were to continue playing bridge. He and one of the officers who, with the soldiers guarding the grounds, had remained behind, sat and watched us.

After what seemed like a hundred years, but was only an hour, a freight car arrived, and the remaining men were told they must also go for questioning, and might each take a small case of clothes. I quickly went down to the bungalow and threw some things into a suitcase for my husband and myself, but when I tried to get on the truck which was waiting outside the front door, a Japanese soldier with a bayonet stopped me.

One of the men, Tiny Rolfe, said he would see me to a nearby house before leaving, but the Japanese immediately got angry, and I begged Tiny to get on the truck before there was any trouble. As it was driven off, the men called out to ask if I was all right, and I croaked rather miserably that I was.

At that moment, seeing the men drive off, and suddenly realizing that my husband might not come back, I was filled with fear. I had stayed in Java, even allowing Jane to go away on a hazardous journey in the care of friends, so as to be near Charles, whom I loved and needed. Now, suddenly, I was totally alone.

It was pitch black outside, and beginning to rain, and as I stood in the lighted doorway with the Japanese officer and the interpreter, I foolishly began to cry. I learned later that there is nothing more annoying to a Japanese than a display of emotion, and I was lucky to have met a fairly lenient officer.

The interpreter told me not to worry, but I said that considering I had one child in England, another heaven knew where, and now my husband taken off to some unknown destination, I had good grounds for feeling miserable.

The officer then apparently asked what I intended to do, so I told him that I would not remain alone in the house – I had unfortunately always been afraid of the dark – and he agreed after some discussion to take me to a Dutchwoman who lived in a house some way down a side road, whom the Britishers had met, though I had not.

We got in his small car, plus interpreter and two soldiers, and drove down a little hill. No lights showed in any of the three houses at the bottom, and I got no answer to my knocking. As the Japanese had been house-searching in the neighbourhood that evening, I could hardly blame the occupants, though I began to get frightened. The car was turned, and started up the hill again, and the rain fell faster.

It was now almost midnight, and the sight of lights showing in a house nearly opposite ours made me ask in desperation if I might try to stay there. The officer, who by this time was getting annoyed, said 'yes', and I went to the door with the interpreter, who knocked. Two Dutchmen came to the door, and the interpreter gave me a push, saying, 'There, these gentlemen will look after you' and promptly left.

The house had been taken over for the staff of British/ Dutch Petroleum, and the three men there, together with Miss Beets, who was the niece of the *Burgemeester* of Bandoeng, were more than kind and looked after me for the next month.

I had locked up our bungalow when I dashed down to fetch my case, but the lights were still blazing in the house, and after an hour or so, there was a violent knocking on the door of the house I was in, and I was sent for. Japanese soldiers shuffled in to search, and I was asked where the British men were. I said they had been collected some hours before, and I did not know where they were. I also asked that the house over the road should be locked up, in case natives went in to loot, and was told to mind my own business, for when Japanese were in charge Indonesians did not do things like that.

At last the Japanese left, and Miss Beets and I went upstairs to try to get some rest, but we could not sleep. Much later, we saw cars stop at our house, and soldiers going in. I was afraid they would come for me again, but nothing happened, and though they scouted round the bungalow, they did not force an entrance.

The next morning Carl van Schagen, who had been with the BPM in both Hong Kong and Singapore and spoke excellent English, went with me and one of the men to see if we could get into the house. I knew the Britishers had about four thousand guilders in a desk drawer in the lounge, which I had forgotten the previous night. The men thought they would remove any drink in the house.

Although we found everything locked up, I remembered there was a pane missing in one of the dining-room windows, and managed to get my hand in and open the lock. On the table were dirty whisky glasses and several copies of *Esquire*. Apparently the Japanese had been enjoying themselves. All drink had been removed, and also the money, but except that the cupboards had been pulled out from the walls and everything searched, the house was as it had been. The two Dutchmen went back over the road, and I got a pail and started to clean the filthy floor, as I did not want to have time to think.

About ten o'clock a large party of Japanese soldiers arrived, shuffling in boots which always appeared several sizes too large for them. They were quite polite, and apparently approved of finding me washing the floor. On asking for the Britishers, and being told they had been taken away many hours before, they appeared satisfied and turned to go. Before they did so, I asked when the men would return, and they grinned and said it would not be long.

The following morning, when I was again over at the house cleaning up, I heard a noise in the garage, and on going out, found a Japanese there. He had arrived in a small car with a native chauffeur, and indicated that he was going to remove the Buick which he found in the garage. I got annoyed, and told him it was Company property, and that he could not do so, whereupon he suddenly turned and spoke to the chauffeur who started the car and drove off. I went back into the house, wondering rather uneasily what was going to happen. I had not long to wait.

First the Japanese, who was in khaki, but not uniform, and later turned out to be from the Secret Police, came into the lounge where I had got down to washing the floor and questioned with signs whether I wanted the telephone mended. It had been cut off the night the men were taken. I asked if I could ring up my husband, and when he would not allow this, told him I didn't need a telephone. He next asked me if I were English, and I answered somewhat brusquely that I was. Suddenly he trotted off to the pantry, rather to my surprise, and came back with a knife. I then realized he was presumably one of the men who had searched the house.

This soon proved to be so, for he told me as he mended the telephone that it was he who had taken the money from the drawer, and that he had written the sum of money on a piece of paper, which he picked up from the desk to show me. The slip had fl.1200 (Dutch guilders) scrawled on it, and I told him that there was more than that, but as I didn't know whether the men had taken any money before locking the drawer, I didn't argue. In any case, it was extremely difficult, as he only knew about two words of English, and my only Japanese was '*Moshi-moshi*' which I learned when we travelled home in 1937 by way of China and Japan, and which I believed meant 'Hello'. I did not dare try it on in case it didn't mean what I thought.

After this little interlude, I continued scrubbing until a car drew up outside, and an interpreter arrived. We sat down, and the following conversation took place through the interpreter:

Q. What are you doing here?

A. I lived formerly in Soebang at the headquarters of a British plantation company. Since Java was invaded by the Japanese, I live here.

Q. Who else lived here?

A. My husband and other British members of the staff, also men from other British companies.

Q. Where are they now?

A. They were taken away two nights ago, and I have been told that they are now in Soeka Miskin prison, outside Bandoeng.

Q. Whose money was in the drawer of the desk?

A. It belonged to the Company for whom my husband worked, and was for the use of the staff evacuated to Bandoeng. (Here I made a bad mistake, and should have said it was mine.)

Q. What staff are they?

A. Dutch and British staff, and their wives and children.

Q. The company is now a Japanese company, and all Indonesians will be provided for. We are not interested in the Dutch staff, and the British are locked up, so the money is now Japanese money. Do you understand?

A. I should like to protest that more money was in the drawer than was written on the slip of paper I have got.

No answer.

Q. How much money have you yourself?

A. About one hundred guilders.

Q. What do you intend to do?

A. Stay here.

Q. And when your money is finished?

A. I shall go down to Bandoeng to friends.

The interview now broke up, and I was left to my own devices. I later learned that I was extremely lucky when the men were first taken away, for those wives who were in Bandoeng with their husbands had in some cases to watch them being pulled out of bed, handcuffed, and taken away. Also, many women living in the town were gated in their homes, whereas for the next six months I was fairly free to do what I wanted, though I was under constant supervision from the civilian Japanese in the surrounding houses, who mainly worked for the Department of Economic Affairs. They were for the most part quiet and well-behaved, unless drunk, and did not interfere either with me or the Dutch who lived in the suburbs and in some cases worked for the Japanese in Government Departments.

For about a month I continued to sleep in the BPM mess, and Carl van Schagen was kindness itself, and always jolly, at least in public. His wife and children had escaped from Singapore to South Africa, and because he had lived for so long amongst the British and had a kindly feeling for them, he helped me endlessly and also lent me money when I had none.

Nevertheless, despite much kindness, after some weeks I felt I must be on my own, especially as one of the men in the mess was violently anti-British. I moved back into our house, and Eunice Blom, a young Dutch girl who, with her English mother, was living in a nearby house, came and slept in the house each night.

She was especially glad to do this, as the Japanese visited the house where she was staying, and she did not like it. When I had washed and mended such clothes as the men had left behind, I was kept busy cleaning the house, and watering and weeding the two gardens as the dry season had commenced.

About two weeks after my husband was interned, I packed a rucksack with a change of clothes for him and for another friend of ours, and walked down to the town to the Heetjansweg, which was the headquarters of the *Kempei Tai* – the Secret Police. This building had already a horrible reputation because of the tortures which had taken place there, and I didn't feel at all comfortable going to it. But as Charles had been without any change of clothes for two weeks, and it had been confirmed that the men were in prison outside Bandoeng, I had to make the effort.

When I got inside the entrance hall I found a long line of children and adults, all clutching parcels of various sizes, standing against one wall. I joined the queue, having bowed to the Japanese in charge, who was bullying everyone as he sat at a table and had each parcel opened in front of him. When he did not like the contents, he threw them out of the window behind him.

When my turn came, I had to undo and repack my rucksack four times, and then he finally decided I could not send it. Luckily at this moment a more cultured Japanese – perhaps also refined at tortures – came in, and asked what was the matter, for the Japanese in charge was yelling at me. The second Japanese listened to my story, and then told me I could send the parcel this once, but must never come back again. I assured him that I would not, and hurried out as fast as I could.

Some little while later, I received a message from Mrs Houwing that a Hungarian friend of hers was going to Soeka Miskin prison to visit a Dutchman (many Dutch senior officials were by then interned with the British), and that it might be a good chance for me to go too. I hurried down the hill, and together with the Hungarian, got into a *sado* (a pony trap, from the word *dos-à-dos*, back to back). We drove the few kilometres out of Bandoeng to the prison.

After knocking on the huge doors, we were eventually admitted to a small room which lay to the right of the entrance, and a Japanese arrived to interrogate us. I had brought some socks and cigarettes for my husband, but at the end of an hour the same conversation had gone round and round: the Japanese looked at the Hungarian, shook his hands together like a boxer, and muttered, 'Very good,' and then he looked at me, and said, 'English, very bad.' Finally he explained to me that if I were to see my husband, which I had asked to do, we should only want to 'Kissie Kissie'. I assured him we shouldn't do anything of the sort in front of him, and then, seeing that I was getting no further, asked permission to leave. Suddenly he said, 'You write letter, I give.' He also took the cigarettes and socks, and actually did deliver the note to my husband.

Later on I went once more to Soeka Miskin, as I heard that the Indonesian Under-Director was reliable, and would take money for the men. Unfortunately, shortly after I had been admitted and was standing in the hall talking to him, after leaving some money, in came some of the extremely nasty members of the *Kempei Tai*, and I shot out like a rabbit whilst the big doors were still open.

Every two or three weeks I walked down to Bandoeng to see many good friends from our Company, and also to see Miss Andrews, who was far from happy, and determined to ask the Japanese authorities to send her back to Sarawak, which she regretted ever leaving. I was not at all keen on this, feeling that the longer we kept out of the way of the Japanese, the better for us, and also, of course, that she had not the faintest chance of being returned.

I was asked at this time to join a Dutch organization to help guerrilla troops who were still in the hills in Java.

I agreed to be used as a letter-box, but refused to do other work, partly because I felt pretty sure I was watched as a suspect Englishwoman living on her own, and also because there was far too much loose talk in the organization, and too many people knew about it.

Two Americans were hidden in the roof of a house

on the road down to the town, and kept there for many months by a Eurasian family. Unfortunately, some Dutch lads had formed an organization which was discovered by the Japanese, and the whole of Tjioemboeloeit was searched and isolated for some days. The Americans tried to escape, and one, I believe, got away. The other hid in an empty air raid shelter and was given up by the woman who owned it.

One night as Eunice and I were sitting in the lounge, there was a knock on the door, and two men came in. One was a young Dutchman, and the other a Scot. Both had escaped from Sumatra, and were in hiding next door. They asked me how I could bear the idea of being interned, but I told them I was short of money and now that my husband was interned, did not particularly mind the idea at all. I certainly saw no sense in giving my Dutch friends trouble by trying to stay free a little longer.

The whole district at that time was full of escaped POWs, and one evening I received a message from the *Burgemeester*'s wife that while she and a friend had been drinking coffee in a café on the Bragaweg, a man in German uniform came up to them, and said he had heard them mention my name, and asked for my address! The women admitted having spoken about me, and he told them a hurried tale that he was really an Australian soldier disguised as a German as he spoke the language perfectly. He had apparently been terribly beaten up by the *Kempei*, then let free, and hoped for help from my husband, whom he said he had met one evening when he was brought to our room in the hotel by one of the Britishers to have a bath.

Since my husband was interned, he hoped to get help from me.

I did remember someone being brought along one evening before the capitulation, but whether the man's name was Smith, or Schmidt, I had no idea. I much disliked European women sitting in the cafés, and in fact later the Japanese printed a notice that it was not fitting they should do so. I sent a message back that if the man genuinely wanted help, he could come up to Tjioemboeloeit and I would see what I could do.

Nothing happened until an afternoon two weeks later, when I had gone upstairs to shower after gardening, and heard a shout from below.

I looked out of my window, and saw what I took to be Chinese itinerant vendors, for one man wore a white suit and the other a plummy coloured European suit and the high round black velvet hat which many Malays wear. I called down that I did not want anything, and was horrorstruck when I was told to come down at once. Then I saw the soldiers at the gate, and realized I had been shouting at the Japanese, and probably the Secret Police, as they were not in uniform.

Slipping into a housecoat I hurried downstairs, only stopping for a moment to warn a friend, Alma Meyer, who was spending the day with me, and had gone to rest after collecting books for some escapers.

When I went onto the verandah I was told to sit down, and the Japanese in the white suit began to question me. The other man, who did not speak at all, sat and watched me. I was asked if I had ever heard of anyone called Smith, or Schmidt, and I must say my tummy turned over about six times. Luckily we had previously had a young Scot called Smith in the Company, and as he had left some years before, I told a long story about him, and how he had gone home and was now working in Ireland. After a bit more questioning, the men got up and the interpreter said they would search the house.

First they found a shorthand book on the desk and got very excited, as they thought it was code, until I explained.

We next went upstairs, and I knocked at Alma's door. We went in. She had just had a letter from her husband, who was a Dutchman working with the Red Cross in Malang, and this was in her handbag. The men looked at the contents, but fortunately gave the bag back to her. Because of the books she was collecting for the Americans down the road, we were both very nervous.

After the Japanese had looked through the other two bedrooms, they opened a cupboard by the stairs and found a lot of men's clothing, including the army boots and uniform which they had left behind when they were interned. I thought I had had it, but explained where the things came from, and nothing more was said.

We went downstairs, and then the second Japanese spoke. I asked what he said, and was told he admired a bowl of marigolds on the desk!

I did not know until some years later that this man was one of the worst of the Secret Police, and that he had just left my husband, whom someone had denounced as a spy, at the *Kempei* headquarters, after torturing him.

It seems incredible to me that anyone should really have given my husband's name, for he never spared himself whilst he was still free, doing all he could, not only for our staff, but for the Army and Air Force with whom he came in considerable contact.

After he had been beaten up, and revived, and beaten again, he was taken down from the pole on which he had been swung, and left. It was during this time that the two Japanese came to see me.

When they returned to the Heetjansweg prison, they put my husband on the back of a motorbike – he could use neither hands nor ankles to grip with – and drove back to Soeka Miskin. Though he expected daily to be taken out for questioning once more, he never again was taken to the Secret Police.

Many thousands of men and women went through much worse tortures, sometimes for weeks on end, in Java and elsewhere. One of the worst things was waiting for the prison door to open day after day, uncertain whether one would be taken away again by the Secret Police for a new going-over.

4

First Camp at Kleine Lengkong

In August, two months after the frightening visit of the Japanese, I took a Dutchman and his wife, Mr and Mrs Heinsius, to stay in the house with me. Mr Heinsius, together with several other members of the Company's staff, was waiting to go back to Soebang to restart work on the plantations under the Japanese. My husband had always hoped that some men would be able to do this, partly to keep up the estates, and partly to get a chance to sabotage Japanese efforts to send away rubber and other products.

At that time the Heinsius had seen few Japanese, and I myself not very many, though I had been shouted at in the street occasionally when a high Japanese was expected to pass. On such occasions, all Europeans had to get off the streets, and others had to turn their backs so as not to look on the Emperor's representative.

I had also met, or rather seen, some of the 'economic' Japanese who lived in our suburb, for one night when I was having supper in the house opposite mine where Eunice had lived, two Japanese came in, dressed in pyjamas, and sat themselves cross-legged in chairs. They picked their toes and drank the gin they had brought with them whilst we tried to continue our meal. It was because of these unwelcome visits that Eunice had been glad to come over and sleep in my house. The Japanese were mostly polite, but when drunk one never knew what they would do.

One night we were ordered a complete blackout, so I warned Mr and Mrs Heinsius to be particularly careful, as there was a secret radio in the district, and I was also watched. By an unfortunate chance, some light showed from their window, and at about eleven-thirty there was a knock on the front door. As I was looking after two large dogs for one of the Dutch managers, I held the dogs whilst Mr Heinsius opened the door.

A Japanese in uniform came in, and, on being questioned, Mr Heinsius explained that he and his wife were only staying with me temporarily till he could get back to the plantations. There was some talk, and then with a shout and a yell, in rushed a second most enraged Japanese, who had apparently been waiting in a car outside. As I was still holding the dogs, I could not bow, and he came over at once and started to kick the beasts with his heavy boots, yelling at me for not bowing.

Mrs Heinsius was ordered downstairs and after shutting the dogs in the kitchen, we were given a rowdy lecture, the main theme of which was, 'No audacity from English,' and 'No British gentlemans behave like that.' We were then ordered to leave Tjioemboeloeit by nine o'clock the next morning, as being unsuitable persons to reside in such a fine locality.

Just as the Japanese were leaving, one of them told me to leave the house key with the Dutchman who lived opposite, who worked for the Municipality. Then I realized that they were ordinary civilian Japanese from the Department of Economic Affairs, but dressed in uniform. I felt a bit better then, and after bowing the Japanese out, told the Heinsius that I would go and see my neighbour early in the morning, and that possibly he might be able to help us, as he knew Japanese and worked for them.

Next morning at seven I went to see him, but to my dismay he told me I should have to go and see the Japanese myself, and apologize. I started up the drive to their bungalow, feeling distinctly nervous.

Before the war Charles and I had spent a very happy weekend with friends of ours who lived in that particular bungalow, but it was with very different feelings that I marched up the drive and knocked on the door.

I gave a message to a servant that I would like to see Colonel Akau, and then, as the minutes lengthened to twenty, my nervousness gave way to irritation, especially as shrieks and yells came from the nearby bedroom, where the Colonel was apparently being assisted in his bath by various lady friends.

Kosaki, the Japanese interpreter who had first come into the house the previous evening, at last came to the door and told me Colonel Akau would not forgive my rudeness. As he had been educated in the High School in Semarang, I was able to speak to him in Dutch. It did not help me to get permission to remain in Tjioemboeloeit. Some ten minutes later, Colonel Akau himself came out, and I told them once again I regretted my impoliteness the previous night, but that it was difficult to hold the dogs and bow, and also we did not usually get visitors so late at night.

After some useless argument, the Japanese still refused to alter his decision, and rather desperately I decided to bluff, and told him that it would be difficult for me to go, as the *Kempei* had ordered me to stay at the house. This was far from the truth, for it was I who had told the *Kempei* I would go on living there when my husband was interned. However, all Japanese whether civilian or otherwise were simply terrified of their own Secret Police, and certainly in this case the bluff worked.

Akau sprang to the door, shouting 'Go! Go! You stay!', and I did my usual disappearing rabbit trick down the drive.

I was delighted with the result, and when some weeks later I was visited one morning by a large party of Japanese and told that I must move out of the house into the little bungalow, I thought I would try the same trick again.

To my amazement I was greeted with roars of laughter, or the nearest Japanese equivalent, which consists of much hissing and sucking in of the breath. When I asked the interpreter what was so funny, he gasped, 'We *Kempei Tai*, and you get out!'

They were exceedingly polite, however, and allowed me to take what clothing the Britishers had left, and a few oddments of furniture, down to the bungalow, and I was given two days to make the change-over. A Japanese from the Ministry of Transport came to live in the house, and except that his Indonesian wives hung over the verandah and jeered at me whenever I carried cans of water from a small stream to water the garden, he was no trouble at all.

Mr Heinsius went back to Soebang just after this, and his wife moved in to Bandoeng. Eunice and her mother then came to live with me, and though our money was getting short, we were really very happy in the bungalow considering the peculiar circumstances in which we were living.

I still had one Company car hidden in the bungalow

garage, but when the Dutch under the leadership of Piet de Vries, who had always handled all the rice business, went back to the plantations, he came one day with the new Japanese head of the Company to collect it. It was to prove invaluable to them, as any form of transport was almost unobtainable.

Whilst the Japanese inspected the car, Piet hurriedly gave me the latest BBC news, and then he went off with his queer little employer. It appeared there was immense competition amongst the Japanese for the job of running our large estates, but the man in charge was quite affable, and left Piet with a great deal of control (and of course all the responsibility if anything went wrong, and someone had to be beaten up or executed).

In September rumours flew round that the British women were to be interned: in fact, those in Batavia had already been interned with their husbands in Struiswijk jail in April, 1942, though in June they were released. To some extent they had the advantage over us, for when they were once again interned, they knew just what to take with them the second time.

On the first Sunday in October, I had the feeling I should be picked up the following day, so I walked down the hill to the Rensinks – he had been manager of Soekamandi sisal estate – picked up my bike from their garage, and rushed on down into Bandoeng to Gerrit and Ita.

For some time our Indonesian servants, at great risk to themselves, had visited me, first bringing Jane's bike which I swopped, and later little presents of charcoal, bananas, etc.

Lastly, Narlin, our second cook, had very bravely managed to get my old Chinese cook out of Soebang, where he had been having a very bad time. The Chinese were often hated by the Indonesians, as they ran much of the rice business in Java then, and all Chinese had consequently suffered.

The old cook lived with us in the bungalow, and I particularly wished to arrange that he, Eunice and her mother might stay on there, and that I might leave what few of the men's possessions I still had in their safekeeping.

When I went hurrying down the hill on my bike to see Gerrit and Ita, they were at first much amused by my presentiment that I was about to be interned, but at last they saw that I was serious, and gladly agreed that Eunice and her mother should continue to use the bungalow. I also arranged with Gerrit that he, too, would keep an eye on old *Kokki* who was pretty ill by this time and got very upset every time he saw me working.

One day he said to me with tears in his eyes, 'No matter old *Kokki* die, but Mem must keep well for children.' The poor old man died two months after I was interned.

I had one other visitor that week, and this was the chauffeur who had driven Jane and the families to Tjilatjap. He appeared at the end of the garden one evening, in a smart white siren suit, and told me that the British women and children had left in a boat, but he did not know its name.

We talked for a while, and I told him I hoped that the war would soon be over, and that we could settle back in Soebang again. I believe I really did expect at that time that Java would be quickly retaken.

At any rate, the chauffeur told me that the Indonesians were leaving their families and going to fight, and at the time I thought he meant to help the Dutch. Since then I have come to the conclusion that he probably meant for the independence of his country. He was apparently working at Kalidjati aerodrome, where the Japanese were making a long concrete runway. He had also no doubt seen, as I had, posters placarded on every lamp-post, showing the Japanese conquest of Asia marked in red, including the northern part of Australia!

Whatever may be said of the Japanese, their conquest was certainly an amazing feat, and their discipline complete – too much so to a British way of thinking. I was often to live in fear of these little men, but seldom hated them, since they seemed largely medieval in their outlook, and were not deliberately retrogressing from a state of culture as were the Germans.

The following evening, Monday, the native *Wedana*, who was the head man of the village, appeared, and I went down the path to ask him if he had come to tell me that I was to be interned. He was a bit staggered, but said it was so, and that he was to spend the night in a shed in the garden to see that I did not run away.

As it began to pour with rain, I told him he need not stay, as I would give him my word not to leave, but his fear of the Japanese was too great to allow him to go away, and he spent a thoroughly uncomfortable night. Meantime, I got busy making a single mattress smaller and thinner, so that I could roll it up with a few unbleached calico sheets which we'd been given, and a blanket, and carry it by a strap.

My few possessions I put in a hat-box, and as many cigarettes and bars of soap as I could lay hands on. I also had a few pieces of jewellery which I eventually slipped into my pocket on leaving Soebang. I handed four things over to Eunice for safekeeping, as she did not expect to be interned, being Dutch. I kept my watch and wedding ring, which I was able to wear throughout internment.

At six o'clock the following morning, after a rather hectic night, Gerrit came puffing up the hill in a freight car he'd made to run on charcoal in place of petrol. When he had spare time he used it to collect patients from estates and bring them in to hospital.

As usual, he was loaded with presents for me, including 100 vitamin tablets – almost unobtainable then – and an army blanket, which I welcomed. I turned down a camp-bed, as I wanted to be able to carry my kit myself. His wife sent boxes of soap, cigarettes, cake, etc., and many kind messages.

I was deeply grateful to them both for all their kindness to me.

Very soon a freight car arrived, and I was ordered to get up on board with the other passengers. These included a young American with her two children, Donald and Phyllis, and an English family consisting of an aged mother, her daughter looking rather like a beauty advertisement – blonde hair, make-up and smart clothes – and a thin grandson of about eight. The grandmother was slightly deranged, and later became a pitiable sight in her unwashed, dirty old wig, down-at-heel shoes, and grubby clothes. Both she and her daughter were to die in later camps, and the boy, who had been allowed to run wild with the servants, caused us trouble by telling tales, peeping through holes in the lavatory doors at the women, and petty thieving. He later joined his father in the men's camp.

I called goodbye to Gerrit, Eunice and her mother, and the old Chinese cook who stood weeping by the kitchen window, and off went the truck at a great speed down the steep hill. We collected some other women and children en route, and shortly before eleven arrived at our first camp.

5

We Face Harsh Reality

Although internment had been hanging over the heads of the women since the previous April, I had somehow thought that when the time came, I should probably be locked up with a few compatriots who had not left Java before the invasion, either in a house or group of houses surrounded by barbed wire, and possibly under guard.

It was therefore something of a shock when our lorry drew up in front of the high bamboo stockade surrounding a broken-down old native schoolhouse, and we were told to get down, and hurried at the point of a bayonet into the office. Japanese officials and native police saw our papers, and checked us in.

Once inside, except for rare visits to an Indonesian dentist or hospital in a guarded, shuttered ambulance, we were not to see the outside world for the next eleven months. Possibly if some of us had realized how cut off we were to be, we might have tried to evade internment, though as our husbands had already been in prison six months and we were many of us short of money, I, at any rate, was glad to have a roof over my head.

All the same, the quarters provided for us were pretty horrifying.

We were in an Indonesian school building which had been condemned as unsuitable for troops. It consisted of six rooms, about twenty by twenty-three feet, placed two by two in an oblong. Each room had an outside and a connecting door, except Room V, which backed on the office, and had only one door.

The floors were tiled, and the high walls were of *bilik*, a plaited bamboo used by the Indonesians for building huts. From a height of about seven or eight feet up to the ceiling there was wire netting on the outer walls of each room, except the two middle rooms. These only had netting on the outer wall, and were consequently very stuffy.

Most of the Jewish women and children, including the wife and daughters of a rabbi, were in these rooms, but did not particularly mind. In the wet season, which started about a month after we were interned, it was quite an advantage, for the rain poured through the netting. Fifteen, and eventually seventeen, people were given space in each room – about six by three feet per person.

A narrow cement verandah with a deep overhanging roof ran round the sides and the back of the building, and had a sunken open drain edging it, which was most dangerous at night in the blackout. The school was surrounded at a distance of some thirty feet by a high *bilik* stockade, with searchlights at each corner and guards.

In the yard at the back of the building a long corrugated iron-covered shed had been erected, and four sunk brick fireplaces made, over which our cooking was done on wood fires. Two tables with long wooden benches stood under the same shed for preparing the food, and the whole place, including the lavatories, swarmed with flies.

These lavatories, which stood at one side of the

building within three yards of the side of the office and Room V, consisted of a row of broken *bilik* sheds, with swinging doors. Each partition contained a cement tank for water, a tin to throw it over one, and a hole in the floor for sanitation. The rest of the floor was covered with wooden slats which had presumably been there for generations of schoolchildren, for they were rotted with worms and filthy with misuse.

At first we were shocked that we should have to squat over a hole, but in fact this probably saved the lives of many people, who would otherwise have died of dysentery through contact with dirty lavatory seats and the like. Five of the sheds were allotted to us, one to the staff and two to the native guards, which were always in a bestial condition.

In the corner between the wash sheds and the kitchen stood an old disused lavatory, which was used as a storeroom, and was later given to us as a 'shop'. Between these two buildings lay a big stone slab with two taps, which we were told we could use for our washing place.

This, then, was to be our home, and it looked sombre enough although the sun was shining and the rainy season still some weeks away. Had we been able to picture it as it would look after two months' rain, I think we would have sat down and howled. As it was, after being passed through the office, and taken by one of the native staff to a room, we began to unroll our mattresses and put down our few possessions.

The Indonesian staff, consisting at that time of a Directrice, two married couples (within a week the two husbands were to become the new No. 1 and No. 2 Directors), one clerk and about six females were, we gathered, to have charge of us. Native police guarded the building, and those off duty sat in a small bamboo hut in front of the office. There was a second hut, very tiny, which was to serve as a hospital.

Just as we were sorting ourselves out, several native soldiers and one of the Japanese came to each room, and said everything was to be left until the luggage had been searched. Since most of the British had already had to evacuate their homes at the time of the invasion, and many others had escaped from Singapore or Sumatra, only to be caught in Java, most of us had very little. I myself had all I possessed in a hat-box, which was to last me, plus gifts from various friends in later camps, for the three years' internment.

Scissors and knives were removed, and later we had to hand in knitting every evening, which was often pulled off the needles each night by the office staff, and it was such petty annoyances, quite apart from the shocking conditions generally, which made us loathe the camp. The fact that most of us had come from comparative freedom outside even in the last unpleasant months, and before that from years in pleasant homes with charming servants, was hard to take. To find ourselves suddenly pitchforked into such a hovel, with strict supervision by an entirely native staff, who had complete control over us, as we quickly learned to our cost, made a most unpleasant impression.

The internees themselves, also, came as somewhat of a shock to me. I had imagined that there were only a few British women left in Java, and suddenly found myself in a camp of about eighty, of whom twenty-five were children ranging from five months to twelve years. What is more, the women were of every race and colour, including Dutch, German, American, French, Italian, Baghdad Jewesses, British Indians. There was even one poor little woman with four tiny children who had come from the Gilbert Islands where, during the First World War, her father-in-law had been interned as a German!

We also had three women, English, Irish and Australian, whose husbands were Dutch, and who should never have been interned with us at all. We tried again and again to get the Japanese to let them out, or, later, to remove them into the Dutch camps which were better than ours, but in vain. Once in, it was practically impossible to get out again, unless one went to work for the Japanese. No Japanese, to my knowledge, ever admitted making a mistake – at any rate when he held the whip hand.

After the initial interrogation and searching of luggage, we were told to hand in to the office what money we had. As I only by then possessed fl.100, this was not difficult. However, many of the women managed to conceal large sums in their luggage, or on themselves, as we were not searched personally, and some were later most generous when times got worse and many of us hadn't a cent.

In the midst of the excitement of women and children having their luggage searched, as they nervously guarded their few possessions, word came that we were to assemble in Room IV to hear a speech by the Japanese commander of the Women's Internment Camps in Java. We were later to find that the British camps varied very much at this time, and one, a 'show' camp at Batoe, in East Java, was to sound a sort of paradise, which indeed compared with the other camps and prisons it probably was.

We crowded into Room IV, and presently in strutted a tiny little officer, followed by his staff. We were told to bow when a Japanese came in, which we did most inefficiently with much giggling. Done once as a form of Japanese politeness, it did not irk me, but when later we were kept bowing as a punishment, for long periods, then it became hateful.

The commandant told us that whilst he regretted that we had to be put in such uncomfortable quarters, there was unfortunately nothing else available in Bandoeng at the time! We should be treated well, and would shortly receive parcels from friends, and everything would be done for our comfort. In the meantime, we were under the control of the Directrice, and there was a staff of some ten men and women who would look after us. It only remained for us to behave ourselves politely, and all would be well.

He then left, and we returned to sit on our mattresses and discuss the situation. Most of the women believed this was a very temporary camp, and that we would be exchanged almost immediately with the Japanese held in Australia. Though optimistic by nature, I was not under any such delusion.

At five o'clock we were called by one of the staff to bring our plates, which were then filled with rice, vegetables, a fried egg and some sauce. Most of us had brought in fruit, bread, butter and some chilli sauce, and although we grumbled at the time, the food during these first weeks was to be the best we were to see for three years, both in quality and quantity.

Some of the adults and children did not like rice, but

the midday and evening meal were really very palatable, and it was only breakfast that took some swallow-
ing. It consisted of small packets of cold rice or tapioca
with a bit of dried fish in the middle, the whole
wrapped up, native fashion, in a banana leaf. After
being kept in the office all night, the sour rice was most
unpleasant to eat.

After some months we got permission to cook sago
porridge for ourselves, and in fact had to take over all
the cooking and work in the camp, as the entire staff,
with the exception of the two male Directors and their
wives, plus one male and one female clerk, were
removed.

The Directrice, a most delightful woman, was unfortunately removed at the end of the first week. Though
she made a very guarded speech before she left, we
gathered – only too rightly as it proved – that she had
been found too kind, and sterner measures were necessary. When months later we asked visiting Japanese
why we were so badly treated, one replied it was
because the British had the impertinence to go on
fighting, and after that we felt better.

In Lengkong there was no radio, but luckily for us,
more women were brought in during the next six
months from whom we were able to learn something of
what was happening in the outside world. Also native
guards on duty round the camp took alternate duty at
Soeka Miskin, the men's prison outside Bandoeng.
Some were bribable with cigarettes, and we occasionally got news of our husbands, though we never knew
if it was true.

On one occasion someone brought in a Malay paper
which the Japanese printed. In it I found to my horror

a notice saying Charles Jackson had been beheaded in Soerabaja the previous week. It was another two months before I knew for certain it was not my husband.

A certain amount was to be learned by poking holes in the *bilik* walls of the office and listening to the staff. Women in the two rooms could do this, but unfortunately not everyone in the camp was trustworthy, and this was even truer as the months went by and more people suffered from starvation. One not only had to watch the spies from the office, but also one or two of the women as well.

During the first weeks in camp, the only work we did was keeping our rooms clean, and as some women had brought in buckets and cloths, this was comparatively easy. Despite the overhanging roof, when the rainy season commenced, and the wind was in the west, the rain poured into our room, soaking blankets and mattresses, which were impossible to dry. Most of us were sleeping on the tiled floor, but were allowed to buy plaited leaf mats from the money taken from us to put under our mattresses, which helped a little to keep out the cold and the damp.

After some months the older women, of whom at least three were seventy, were allowed to buy bamboo *bali-balis* (pallets) which enabled them to sleep off the ground, besides providing somewhere to sit and storage space under the bench for their luggage. Otherwise no chairs or tables were at first allowed in the camp, though a few backless benches had been placed outside the rooms on the narrow verandah, and in the kitchen shed.

The ground round the school was mainly mud and pebbles, some twenty feet wide. Over the top of the high bamboo palisades we could see the sky. We were in the centre of Bandoeng. As the Japanese trained Indonesians as soldiers, large parties stomped round outside the camp in the evenings, singing in Malay about the downfall of the English and the Americans.

Within a few days of internment, we organized ourselves as best we could. Some women cleaned rooms, some went on duty to help prepare vegetables for the midday meal, and I started a school as the children rapidly got out of hand.

Each room had a narrow plank shelf running round it about five feet from the ground, and a small length was allotted to each internee, on which to keep treasured personal possessions. Any clothes were kept in the owner's case, and some of the women with children had come into camp with anything up to two or three steel trunks or cases. There was endless argument about how much room each should have, and in fact there was a never-ending bickering between some mothers and the women without children.

Another bone of contention was the lack of discipline amongst some of the children, and it was for this reason I started the school at Lengkong as soon as I could. At first the new Indonesian Director refused to allow it, but after a struggle he gave in. Together with Ellie Benson, who was the Dutch daughter of Corrie Meyer but married to an Englishman, and who took on the under-fives, I ran two classes for the older children.

Considering the trouble I had to get permission to start the school, we were much amused as the months went by to find that the Director always brought visiting Japanese to see the 'school'. I bought a notebook for each child (which eventually had to last our months in Lengkong), and was fortunately able to borrow some lesson books from Dutch and British mothers. Only two of the older children wrote English, although this was a British internment camp, as they had attended Dutch schools. So for the first months I had to teach them in rather shaky Dutch, which amused the children enormously. Later, through hearing the adults speaking English, and with a few extra lessons, they soon learned to speak excellently, and four or five of the older ones could write a really good essay in English at the end of eleven months.

When they did well, they were allowed to look at a large book showing paintings in the National Gallery in London, and probably knew more about those paintings than most British children!

As a school no doubt it would not have passed a very high standard, but we all felt that discipline of some sort was necessary for the children, who were liable to get out of hand soon enough.

One or two of the boys were troublesome, especially Benny Raymond, one of the Jewish group. He was a helpful enough little imp, and I was very fond of him, but at eleven he was far too mature, and at times when it suited him could be very deceitful. Part of the trouble was that the mothers condoned stealing, either from the natives or Japanese, by their children, and though in later camps it certainly was necessary to steal firewood and other things to survive, I always thought it should only be done by the women.

This may have been a larger problem in Java and Sumatra than elsewhere out East, as the camps were full of children. Another difficulty in the later camps, when we were put with the newly-interned Dutch, was their dislike of any form of boarding school and firm belief in home influence only. Mothers continually lied to the Japanese to keep their sons with them, even at seventeen or eighteen, instead of letting them go either with their fathers, or in special camps. Eventually all males, except the very aged and boys under ten or eleven, were segregated. It was certainly a very good thing when they were moved from the older women's camps, as we found in later prisons.

When it was nearing Christmas, 1942, a notice was put on the board at the back of the camp, saying that in future we must prepare our own food, and squads of women must be ready daily at 9 A.M. We still had a coolie who came in each morning to light the fires and prepare tea water, and as he never did this before 8.30 A.M., it was manifestly impossible for the mothers to see to their children, and be ready for work at nine.

Early one morning Emmy Starkey, a Swiss friend who was married to a British geologist, and I were out washing our clothes on the slab by the lavatories. Emmy and I had been grumbling about the new rules, which also stated we must in future unload all food and vegetable trucks. As I finished my washing, Emmy called that it would be better if we complained to the Japanese, though she herself had been trying to get in touch with the Red Cross or the Swiss Consul for weeks without success.

I went up to the Director's wife, who had been standing listening to our conversation, and asked if it were possible to have an allowance of charcoal so that mothers could prepare some porridge for their children early each morning, and thus be on time for work at nine. Although I had been careful to bow before speaking, and of course spoke in Malay which is somewhat like Indonesian, she flew into a terrific temper, and rudely told me it was quite impossible.

Afterwards I heard from Room V women that she and the No. 1 Director had nearly come to blows the previous night as she tried to stop him going off to see a sweetheart of his. He went, and no doubt the wife was frightened that the Japanese would pay a surprise visit in his absence, as they often did, which would mean severe punishment for them both. Unfortunately I did not know this at the time, or I might have waited for a more propitious moment.

Quite unaware of the brewing storm, I came round the side of the building, after hanging up my washing, to find Emmy being beaten up by the Director's wife with a broom handle. The native police were called, and the offender was put in the police box.

By this time the Director, who was rather tall and thin for an Indonesian, and who had previously been chosen for his fanatical hatred of Europeans, especially women, came to the door of the other office. I went up to him to say it was I, not Mrs Starkey, who had asked for charcoal. He immediately landed me a blow across my face, and, when I asked him how he dare do that, came down the steps after me, tripping over a child's pram in the rush. By this time a group of women and children had come to the door of Rooms I and II, and it says a lot for our fear of the staff, and the head Director in particular, that not one of us laughed until many hours later.

As the Director was by this time gibbering and appeared to have gone quite mad, the native police joined in, and warned us not to hit back. Ellie Benson was the next to be caught, and we were both put into the police box with Emmy to await punishment.

We insisted that we must see the police, or a senior Japanese, and I must say this was done with sinking hearts, as we all had a pretty good idea what Japanese punishment entailed. Still, it was no good letting the staff get away with knocking us about, and after the Director had rushed round the camp with a revolver in his hand, asking if anyone else wanted punishment, the camp settled down rather tensely to await the arrival of the Japanese.

About eleven o'clock, after several false alarms, the chief of police – a plump Indonesian who had so far been fairly kind to us – arrived, with a Japanese officer. The native staff poured out their tale first, and then we prisoners were taken into the office. We were told we had been insubordinate, impolite and generally a trouble in the camp. The interpreter told us he had been badly beaten when a prisoner in Australia, and lost all his teeth. What we needed was a spell in dark cells.

We replied we did not think this would be a good thing for the women and children, and that we had always been polite and bowed to the staff, but we did not see why they had any right to hit us. Also we did not consider the No. 1 Director, or the wife of the No. 2 Director (who was a sadist of the most unpleasant type), were suitable people to be in charge of us. After some argument, we were sent back to the police box, and the Japanese got up and left without saying a word.

–

The staff were furious that we had been given no punishment, and we were kept in the police box all day, though this we did not mind so much as it gave us a chance to try to pump the police for news. Most of the camp too rallied behind us, and gave us what food they had, and some cards, so we played three-handed bridge.

During the long, hot afternoon when we were all looking rather haggard and dishevelled, a car drove up outside, and two civilian Japanese and Noel Foster, one of the young Company accountants, who was in prison with my husband, came in. I was called to the office, whilst the staff looked on in eager anticipation of fresh trouble, but the Japanese were quite pleasant, and only asked me about the money which had been left by the Britishers when they were taken away from the hill house.

I told what had happened, and fortunately was able to produce the slip of paper which the Japanese had given me, and luckily the two Japanese agreed that my story was correct.

The 'economic' Japanese, like those who lived up in Tjioemboeloeit, were usually extremely polite, and these two were no exception to the rule. They even allowed me to ask about my husband and the other men, and as at that time no one had died, we all felt very pleased with the visit, especially after such a dreadful start to the day.

I was a little afraid that Noel might mention to my husband when he got back to the prison that we had been brought from the police box, but he either didn't notice it, or didn't mention it. He himself looked neat as a new pin, though probably in borrowed garments.

Emmy, Ellie and I were kept till nine at night in custody, and then taken under guard to our rooms. The following morning one of the staff called us to appear in the office, and judging by the grins, something unpleasant had been cooked up for us. Emmy Starkey, who was over fifty, had to get down and scrub the office floor, Ellie was detailed off to clean the hospital hut, and I was told to clean out the lavatories, including the ones used by the staff and soldiers.

As I had no brush, I had to scrape the whole filthy place, which had apparently never been cleaned before, with half a coconut shell. Both Emmy and I, who were within call of one another, tried to sing, but the office staff stood over her making her do pieces of floor again and again, and I was crying with rage among the filth. The more I cried, the more the old soldier in charge of me cried. It really was ludicrous, though my sense of humour was slightly warped at that moment, especially when I came to the two sheds used by the soldiers, and found that they had stuffed some contraceptive sheaths into the holes, much to the amusement of the office staff, who stood watching and giggling.

Luckily we still had a bit of carbolic soap, and were able to wash afterwards, before being put back in the police box. When we were let out that night, we had to bow about thirty times to the Director which made Emmy Starkey faint, after which we were allowed to return to our room.

The following day we were taken to the police box once more, but this was the last day of our punishment, for which we were heartily thankful.

All this happened just before Christmas, and up to that time we had had reasonable food, and not too much work. Those who had money were still allowed to buy extra fruit, milk and occasional chocolate, and also to buy cottons, toothbrushes, and other necessities. Unfortunately, at Christmas conditions became much harder.

In the first place, religious services, which up to then had been held weekly by Protestants and Catholics in the camp each Sunday, were stopped. The Japanese refused to allow any further gatherings of more than two or three people even inside the camp.

We were also told to provide two unattached (without children) women at 7 A.M. to prepare the sago porridge which we were by then allowed in place of the horrible sour rice packages which had been served in the beginning.

We still had blackouts each night, so it meant preparing the grated coconut in the dark, and then cooking the lumps of dirty brown sugar, together with sago and coconut, as soon as we were able to light the fires with wet wood. The cooking had to be done in large iron 'saucers', which the Indonesians use for all cooking, and as long as they had handles on the sides it was not too bad. Those *wadjangs* without, which measured some two and a half feet across, were very dangerous to handle, especially when full of a boiling, glutinous mixture.

Another anxiety was lifting off the huge rice 'kettle', which was really a large tar drum in which we had to cook the rice for the whole camp. It was filled one third full of water, then had a wooden steamer put in, and finally the washed rice. The weight when the rice was cooked was colossal. A bamboo pole was then slung through the two wobbly ears or rings at the top, and then, with two women shouldering the pole on each side of the drum, it had to be lifted off the sunken fire. Since we saved our good shoes 'to go out of camp' and wore *klompen* (wooden soles with a rubber or cloth strap over the foot) it was very hard to stand steadily to take the full weight of the drum.

Fortunately we were mostly fairly healthy, and each afternoon had a gymnastics class, both in Lengkong and later in prison. I also taught the children gymnastics and dances I knew, till eventually we became too ill and tired to carry on.

Nevertheless, despite all the difficulties of cooking, unpleasant staff and conditions, the feeling in Lengkong was better than in any other camp I was to live in. Probably because we were newly interned and still kept fairly healthy with vitamins and tablets, which most of us had brought in with us, and also because of Bandoeng's cool climate.

Otherwise, the shocking conditions of the camp would have led to many deaths; whereas at the end of eleven months, although we had several cases of illness, with very sporadic, if any, medical attention, no one died.

6

Last Months in Bandoeng

At the end of May I gave the children a holiday from lessons for two weeks, as we had used up all our exercise letter books. I had no money left to buy any more, so it was necessary to rub them all out so that they could be used again.

After one or two days I took over the nursing of an urgent case in the little hut used for a 'hospital'. The doctors changed continually, mostly because they were found to be sympathetic when they occasionally came. Finally we had an old Indonesian, who popped his head round the door of the stockade each day, saying, 'Sorry, ladies, no time today.'

Ena Bouchard, the woman I was to look after, was one of three women in camp married to Dutchmen who were wrongly interned with us. Ena, an Irishwoman, was a particularly bad case as her husband had only gone back to work for the Japanese on the Sumatra oilfields on the understanding that his wife should receive one hundred guilders a month, and not be interned, as she was not strong.

The moment he left for Sumatra, Ena was interned with the British, and this at a time when only a small number of high Dutch officials were interned at all. The injustice of it, and the fact that she received no money at all, made her ill, and she started having very unpleasant fits. These seemed to me to be brought on by her mental state, but became aggravated by having to share a room with sixteen women and children, and the fact that the moment she started a fit, all the native staff came and stared at her.

After some time her condition became so bad that the doctor did sometimes come and give her an injection, but she came to rely on this, and when he could not be reached, her condition got worse, with heart and pulse growing weaker. Eventually we persuaded the Director to allow her to be in the 'hospital' under my care, on the understanding that I was responsible for her, and that no Indonesian staff were to crowd into the tiny room if she was ill.

It seemed likely that as Ena never had convulsions at night, there could be nothing radically wrong, and after some ten days' rest, and somewhat firm treatment, she eventually came out of the depression. For her amusement I started to write plays, so that she might guess from act to act how the play would work out, and we had quite a lot of fun over this.

The lack of medical attention in the camp was only one of our worries. The conditions in the rooms, however much we cleaned, got worse. In many cases the mothers with young children all slept together on the same mattress, both to keep warm and take less room – as more internees were brought in, our space got less and less.

We were allowed out of the rooms to go to the lavatory sheds at night, but many people had dysentery and bladder trouble, and others were frightened of the native police who patrolled round the inside of the camp at night. As the children got more nervous, they wetted their beds, so that the stench sometimes in the crowded rooms was dreadful. During the rainy season from

October to March there was no means of drying and airing the mattresses, and even in the dry season only a small number could go out daily on the racks built on one of our last remaining bits of space. Each room had a turn every fifth day, but only when it was fine. We were also prohibited from hanging washing or airing mattresses whenever a Japanese was expected to visit the camp and inspect.

After a time we settled down into various cliques in the camp. Everyone worked well together with very little friction for general purposes, and we spent what spare time we had sewing, reading and writing, though shortage of both books and paper caused much distress.

When we were first interned most of us brought in one or two books, with the idea we should receive books and parcels from outside. This, alas, never happened, and at the end of six months most of us had read the hundred or so books several times. Unfortunately I had not taken a copy of Shakespeare when I left Soebang, but I had a copy of Julian Huxley's *Essays of a Biologist*, which became very popular. Also, when Miss Andrews was later brought into camp, the Dutchwoman who had offered her a home in Tjioemboeloeit most kindly sent me R. N. D. Wilson's beautiful book of one hundred National and Tate Gallery pictures, which later became such a godsend for the children in the school.

The head of the camp, Madame Caly, was a most interesting woman who had married an Englishman and lived in both Alexandria and the Lebanon many years previously. She was Dutch by birth, and when widowed came to live in Java with her small son, and settled in Bandoeng where she did French and Italian translations, and gave language lessons.

For some time in Lengkong Ellie Benson and I had French lessons with her in the evening, using a Dutch/French grammar. Occasionally we amused ourselves taking rude *dictée* about the Japanese, or the expected arrival of the Americans. As all books had to be handed in to the office each evening it was just as well our efforts were not understood.

Each night at ten o'clock we all had to be in our rooms, and the Director, or his wife, with two or three native soldiers, came round each room. A head had been chosen for each apartment, and it was her job to check the occupants and tell the Indonesian if correct; also, if anyone was lying down, why they were doing so and not bowing.

The children, after some weeks of argument, were allowed to sleep, though as at first, we had to have unshaded overhead light, they often could not do so.

After a time we did get permission to shade the light, and this did help some of us to sleep, though the night was usually disturbed with people going out to the back, children crying or wetting their beds, or having nightmares, and of course by the few who snored happily through the night!

The second Director, unlike his superior, was a fat little man who had probably at one time been a clerk in an office. He bore us no ill will, nor we him, and sometimes he used to converse quite pleasantly, and tell us we were better off inside. At the time I thought he was fooling us, but later found that what he said was true, and that outside thousands of Indonesians had pitiful distribution of food, no soap and practically no clothes, so that some had to dress in paper or sacks, if they could obtain them.

His wife was a cruel, dominating woman, as I mentioned previously, and something of a sadist. Her great amusement was to make us bow many times when she came to check up the rooms at night. Beautifully dressed in her smartest *sarong* and *badjoe* (little jacket), she afterwards talked outside our doors to the police guards, inciting them to go in and cut off our ears, or beat us up. This maybe sounds silly now, but we were then completely at the mercy of these people. For months many of us slept with any bit of iron bar or broken knife we could steal, which we carefully hid in our mattresses during the day.

In fact we could have done little enough if the guards had decided to come into the room, as there was no easy way we could block up the doors, and in any case those with dysentery had to be able to get out. The Japanese, too, came round the camp occasionally at night, and would of course have been furious if the doors had been fastened in any way.

The only Japanese who ever came into the room late at night mistook us for the brothel which we gathered was on the opposite side of the street. One came drunkenly staggering in one night, and was either so impressed or frightened by Emmy Starkey shouting at him in the gloom that he left precipitately.

As time went by, and the food and conditions of work got harder, many of the young girls between eleven and sixteen showed the strain. They were mainly daughters of the Jewish families in Rooms II and IV, and for some reason the natives bullied them more than anyone else. The second Director's wife would call out one or other of them to the police box during

the day, and then tell the police that these girls should
be getting married but no one would have them. Then
she poked at them and showed off their good points, and
made them suffer many indignities. They also had to
take turns to carry hot water to the Director in the office
each morning, so that he could shave. If anything was
wanted, they were the ones to be called to the office.

This was partly because they had been brought up in
Java and spoke Malay, and some even spoke Soendanese, the language of West Java. Perhaps because
they were gentle and timid, they got worse treatment,
as is so often the case when bullies are in power.

Two of the girls, however, were of a very different
type. Their mother, Mrs Baher, had originally come
from Baghdad, and until his death her husband had
been the rabbi in Bandoeng. Sybil and Helene had both
had an excellent education, and cooked and waited on
their mother endlessly. Although she later became very
ill, she continually fought with both girls, for she was
of the old school and expected her daughters to marry
the husband of her choice when they were still very
young. This both girls had refused to do.

I liked the old lady, despite her temper, and tried to
get her to understand that once the girls had been
allowed a modern Dutch education, she could hardly
expect them to go back to the old idea in Jewish
families, and sit at home until she married them off.
Sometimes she got angry at their eating camp food, but
here again, they worked as hard as anyone and had to
eat what there was.

Mrs Baher herself only did a little vegetable preparation, and in the beginning was allowed to pay for
special food to be brought in for her, but this only

lasted for a few months. She had masses of luggage, and had brought plenty of tinned stuff with her, also money, so for the time was able to manage.

It was quite impossible to expect the girls to eat special food, even if they had got it, for it all meant extra cooking, and we were only allowed a small amount of charcoal per person, for heating water, cooking, etc. The Indian and Jewish women immediately started to make jams, sweets, etc., which they bartered, and it was amazing to us at that time to find out how much could be cooked in a little iron *wadjang* on a charcoal fire.

It was a blessing we did have a few small stoves, as during the wet season the rain poured into the bottom of the cooking trenches, sometimes to a depth of one or two feet, and as we were never allowed by the native staff to cover the wood pile, it was weary work trying to get the wet wood going for a fire. The smoke poured out over the camp and into the rooms, where children and grown-ups sat shivering and choking among the wet mattresses.

Luckily for us the last months in Lengkong were in the dry season, as I doubt whether many of the small children could have stood a second winter in such damp and cold conditions.

From May onwards, our treatment became more severe, and we had to practise blackouts. During these we were gated in our rooms, without light, and usually spent the time singing, or forming vocal orchestras, much to the annoyance of the staff and guards. Since we were not actually breaking the rules, they could not stop us.

We also had singsongs on the narrow verandah in

the evenings, hoping that people outside the camp would tell our Dutch friends who were still free and able to visit Soeka Miskin. We hoped by this means to convey to the men we were full of beans, and I suppose, compared with the months to follow, we were.

One night there was an eclipse, of which Indonesians are excessively superstitious. Whenever any staff dared to come round, we talked in loud voices of what the gods were doing to wicked people who shut us up and treated us so badly. How we did enjoy their terrified faces!

The older women, including Madame Caly, a Mrs Noordhoek Hegt who was always calm and kind, old Granny Arden and many others, bore up amazingly in all the squalor. During the hot afternoons in May we were punished if we lay down in the afternoon, so when there was no work we had to sit back to back on the narrow benches outside, despite the glaring sun. The sweat poured down where our backs touched, but it was better than no support at all. The sufferers from lumbago and sciatica in the wet weather found it impossible to squat on the floor in the heat.

Elvira Pugh, a cultured Dutchwoman, of mixed birth, married to a man in Shell, was a great help at this time. Like so many of the mixed families of Java, she had gentle, sweet manners, and great intelligence. She had studied widely, and was particularly interested in art, and had spent much time as a journalist travelling in Europe. We really did spend happy afternoons planning trips in Italy, France and other countries I should visit, discussing what I should see, which kept me enthralled for hours. Elvira had a lot of pleasure from the National Gallery book, and together with Emmy

Starkey, we spent afternoons and evenings making plans for future travels. In this way we could escape from the filth, noise and lack of privacy which affected all of us, but Elvira most of all.

Though conditions were bad, after some argument we got the Japanese to agree to our having a shop. Sybil Baher and I ran it in our spare time, and she and I worked happily together in later camps too. The shop really consisted of rations which had to be divided out in the camp, and included soap (much needed as our supplies were finished), fruit, native tobacco to roll into cigarettes, jam in cellophane packs, and such things as wooden *klompen* which we all wore as the ground was so filthy. Also cotton, needles and wool.

Sybil and I had permission from the Japanese to use the office typewriters to keep the lists and accounts for the shop. As the native office clerk was a beginner, we had the most childish pleasure in dashing off our own typed lists in grand style, much to his annoyance.

Towards the end of August, 1943, rumours again started that we were to leave Lengkong and join our husbands. Some did not believe this at first, but I suddenly felt sure we would leave on 8 September. Why I should have felt this, I do not know, as I never again had the same certainty. It did happen to be true, as listeners through a hole in the office *bilik* heard, but we were never given any orders to pack. The staff were absolutely stunned when we began to get ready to leave on the 8th! We were given a huge feed, and kept in readiness all day, but the train from Soerabaja, which we were to join, was late. In the end we did not see the last of Kleine Lengkong till 2 A.M. on 9 September.

With a few exceptions – timid souls who thought any change must be for the worse – we were as glad to see the last of the No. 1 Director as he no doubt was of us. However, we were to find on reaching our destination that the names of those of us who had been in trouble were already entered on a 'black list'.

Everyone was loaded up with bundles and parcels, buckets and frying-pans, and all sorts of oddments. From the beginning of internment I had used my husband's tweed coat, which kept me warm and reminded me of him, as a sort of mobile cupboard, and all the pockets were invaluable. Scissors and knives had to be left behind, to our rage, but luckily I had a pair of surgical scissors which broke in two parts, and I had so far been able to hide them in my mattress.

We piled into the waiting buses, and were taken through the blackout in pouring rain to the station. There we squatted on the cold, ill-lit platform until the Soerabaja train came in at about 5.30 A.M. Along the platform from us was a party of Chinese who were being moved from Soeka Miskin, and when the train started Elvira and I got in the same coach with them, but were quickly turned out. I cannot say enough for the Chinese with whom I came in contact, for they did their best to supply us with food, help and information wherever possible, and made the lot of many British interned in Java much lighter.

Finally, at 6 A.M., the long train of shuttered wooden trucks pulled out of the station, and we were on our way to yet another unknown destination.

7

Tanah Tinggi Prison

The part of the train in which the internees from Bandoeng travelled was fourth class ('tenth class' according to one of the Japanese guards!), and had wooden benches along each side, and another bench running up the centre of the truck. I was sitting with one of Lydia Leslie's twins on my knee – she was the Dutch girl married to a Scot who had declined to leave Soebang with the other British women – and we were all packed in like sardines. Just as well, as it turned out, for there was no back to the centre seat, and it would have been impossible to keep one's balance round the huge hairpin bends if we had not been squeezed so tight.

We stopped at one station – Poerwakarta – which lay some fifteen miles from the great plantation company where I had spent so many happy years, and were allowed to buy a little fruit.

The other trucks were full of women and children from British camps in East Java, and they had been travelling three days and nights already in stifling, shuttered coaches. Some of the children had fever, and there was a terrible shortage of water.

When the train had stopped in Bandoeng, I had seen a friend, and tried to have a word with her, but the guards immediately shouted at us. As usual news seemed to filter through about where we were going, though no one knew. Each time someone tried to open a shutter, a guard pushed into the crowded truck and yelled to have it shut. As the morning wore on and we came down into the coastal plain, the heat became suffocating.

After what seemed an interminable journey we arrived at Meester Cornelis station, on the outskirts of Batavia. We were given water, some rice wrapped in a banana leaf, plus a banana. The long train waited in the blazing sun whilst the Chinese were taken away, then shunted into a siding, and finally on to Tangarang station. From there we were loaded into open lorries and moved off to Tanah Tinggi prison.

When Java was invaded by the British during the Napoleonic Wars, under General Gillespie, a battle was fought at Tangarang. The British General might well have been horrified if he could have seen how his countrywomen were treated there one hundred and twenty years later!

Tanah Tinggi prison was built on the usual Dutch plan, that is to say, star-shaped, though this prison, unlike Soeka Miskin, was single-storey and we had no water laid on in the cells.

When we arrived in the boiling heat we were told to wait in a central triangular courtyard until all the lorries arrived. Near where I sat on the edge of a tiled verandah was the punishment cell, which had an iron trap-door with a grating under which the prisoner had to crawl to get into a small dark kennel. In Tanah Tinggi whilst we were there such cells were used for the criminals only, but Bertie van Mook, the wife of the acting Governor General who was ordered to leave Java before the Japanese arrived, was put in such a tunnel with several men for weeks, with no sanitation, and food pushed in through the hole in a tin. The Japanese were furious to find Dr van Mook had escaped, so punished his wife, whom I knew in a later camp. When she was let out of the hole her young son and daughter didn't know her, she had become so thin and haggard.

When all the train trucks were empty, all the internees had to walk round and round in the blazing sun in the triangle. Under one large tree the new staff and guards sat and laughed at us. In one corner was a whipping block which had apparently been used for former prisoners.

Most of the women and children by this time were parched with thirst and utterly exhausted. Many women fainted, much to the annoyance of the Japanese, who did not believe in illness.

It appeared that internees from Semarang and Cheribon in mid-Java had arrived some days before, and had been put to clean the quadrangle which had previously been used by the criminals and was absolutely filthy. One small side room had been turned into a hospital, but the first-comers had been locked in one room till after our arrival.

The criminals themselves had been moved to an adjoining block, and at first did the cooking and work in the camp. They were certainly some of the most sinister characters I have ever seen, and upset many of the women at night by beating on the cell walls and screaming. Also we could hear when they were beaten up by the guards, and it was horrible.

Our triangular block of the prison had cells on two sides of a high, tiled corridor, whilst the third side was divided into two huge barrack-like rooms, and a washroom which just had some taps on each wall. The lavatory was a similar high-ceilinged room with a long trench in the floor and a pole stretched about one and a half feet over the top which you held on to whilst you squatted to perform. As the edge of the trench soon got befouled you had to watch out you did not slide down into the muck. The open drain went through other parts of the prison before it reached us.

Our section of the prison was run by a Mrs Washington, said to be a German, and a part-Indonesian Director plus Indonesian wardresses. The whole camp was under a Japanese commandant, though we saw little of him or his staff after the first few days, except when officials visited the wing.

During our parade in the triangular forecourt, we were called in turn to give our names and particulars to the Indonesian Director, who sat with other officials under the trees in the centre of the triangle.

By five o'clock we were allowed to fall out, and sit on the edge of the blazing hot tiled verandah, with our feet in the gutter, waiting to be allotted a cell or place in one of the large rooms.

All the luggage was brought in – the women from other camps seemed to have an amazing amount – and was dumped in the central part, and we got busy carrying it to its owners, many of whom were far too ill to move. We had been warned on our arrival not to drink water out of the taps, but most of us were too thirsty to heed the warning, though we were to regret our foolishness before long.

The cells along the two sides were eight by five feet, and contained a plank bed, a tin dipper and a bucket which could be used for sanitation or washing oneself or clothes. Doors to the cells were iron half-way up, and then barred, and as we were forbidden to hang anything over the bars, the cells were cold and damp in the rainy season, and wardresses and Japanese could, and did, look in at any time of the day or night.

On the third side of the triangle the largest room rapidly became known as the fish market, for about a hundred and fifty mothers and children were locked in each night from 7 P.M. to 7.30 A.M., with only one hole in the floor for sanitation. Bamboo platforms ran the length of each room, with two more platforms down the centre, each about two feet from the ground, and on these the internees slept. As they were built on unsplit bamboo poles, forbidden by the Dutch latterly because rats so often nested in the hollows and caused plague, the outlook from a hygiene point of view was not happy.

Next to the fish market was the revolting lavatory, and the washroom, and lastly another fairly large room with a well tiled floor, and wooden planks raised on blocks at one end for beds. It was much easier to keep clean than any other room and was much sought after.

The tiled corridor which ran round in front of the cells and rooms was about five feet wide, with a drop of some two feet to the cement gutter. Later it became very dangerous when mothers and young children were moved on protest from the fish market into cells. Apart from the rooms on the triangle, we were also given three rooms and a washroom through a door in one wall past the cleanest room. This had already been taken by women from the Salvation Army and a few helpers for a small hospital. Those rooms were supplied with hospital beds, and were both clean and quiet compared with the bedlam in the rest of the camp.

Whilst I was helping to move trunks and cases from the courtyard, I came across a young woman, lugging a baby in a carrycot, who was later to become a great friend. On the afternoon of our arrival at Tanah Tinggi, however, she was practically in a state of stupor, trying to collect her luggage and look after her baby, who was then about a year old.

Deborah Pope had decided to stay with her husband on an East Java estate when war came, although she was expecting a baby and was not well. I think she was wrong, but besides being one of the bravest women I have ever met, she was also the most stubborn, and so she stayed.

She was ill after the birth of Ferne, and was allowed to stay in a Swiss clinic in East Java for a year. When all the British were to be moved to West Java, she had to come too. That is how I found her, completely exhausted after a terrible four-day journey without food or water in the shuttered train.

As Deborah was pretty well at the end of her tether, she was allowed a cell with her baby Ferne, instead of being put in the fish market.

When we were finally locked up for the night, I was in a cell three doors along from her, with Emmy and Elvira in between. Unfortunately I soon began to feel ill from having drunk the tap water, and started an attack of bacillary dysentery. I tried to get the wardress who passed from time to time to let me out as my bucket was soon overflowing, but she refused. Finally I was past caring and too weak to move, so I lay on my plank, completely foul. This was the only time I would have been glad to die, especially next morning when the cells were unlocked, and Emmy and Elvira got me to hospital, and cleaned up the filthy mess in my cell. The following day I was thankful to be able to return, for the hospital was overcrowded with many patients far more sick than I was, and luckily I recovered quickly.

Many people, I know, found it intolerable to be locked alone in a cell for many hours. For some of us it was the only taste of privacy for a year, and I was never so happy as when the door was locked each evening, and I settled down to play patience with an old pack of cards to see when I would get out of camp, or tried to read by the dim ceiling lamp.

Alas, our beautiful peace did not last long, and Elvira, Emmy and I were moved to the comparatively clean room which, except for lack of sanitation, was not too bad. Mothers with one child, and sometimes a friend, were in one row of cells, and the sick or mothers with several children were in the second row. It was understandable they wanted to have a small 'family' place, but when there were four or five children and mother to share plank and soiled mattress, the cells got both dirty and smelly. Fortunately after a time the cells were left unlocked at night (they were locked by one main switch, which gave us an added sense of claustrophobia), and people could go to the lavatory.

Not many dared do this, as the prison was reputed to be haunted, as it well might have been. One ghost was a soldier who stood outside the lavatory door, bound to the wall by a leg-iron. It was amazing on a moonlight night how often something white was by that door. The second, and more disconcerting ghost was a Chinese who had committed suicide in one of the cells. We should probably never have heard of him had it not been for a strange occurrence.

Vena Versloot, a Newcastle girl married to a Dutchman, and one of the three wives who should not have been interned with us, had a jolly little son, Ronnie. They were both delighted when they had a cell of their own. However, on the first night the child woke the whole block by screaming during the night and nothing would quieten him. The same thing happened the following night, and he said there was a man hanging in the doorway making horrible faces at him. Nothing would alter his exact description, and eventually a wardress explained that a Chinese had committed suicide by hanging himself with his pyjama cord from the door. Vena and Ronnie were moved to another cell, and there was no further trouble.

The whole atmosphere in this dark and gloomy prison was very bad. An Egyptian woman, married to a Dutchman, was brought in with us for angering the Japanese by saying she could see the war would end in August some year soon, and there would follow worse bloodshed. One day Farida sent her beautiful young daughter – who had to look after her carefully all the time as she fell into trances in the most unexpected places – to ask me to go to her cell. She told me when I got there that 'a black cloud which had been hanging over me' would go. My husband and children were safe, and after the war I would have a son with an unusual name. When this happened, we were to go to a church and give thanks. I was particularly staggered by her message, as it followed the prediction given by the little woman in Putney! I must say I thought it extremely unlikely I should ever have another child, though I did.

On another occasion Farida warned Deborah that little Ferne would fall in the stone corridor and hurt her head. When that happened (and despite all our care it did) she was to be called. Farida placed a small stone under the child's head to cure the concussion, and Ferne certainly got over the fall at once.

Although most of the people interned were British – with some Americans, one or two Dutchwomen were brought in as punishment, either because their husbands were in high positions or because the women had annoyed the Japanese. One such was Mrs Tjarda van Starkembourg Stachouwer, the American wife of the former Governor General, and her younger daughter – both of whom had stayed with us at the Big House in Soebang. She was a quiet woman, an intellectual, and spent much of her time sitting on a stool in the triangle. She and her daughter each had their own cell, and it took some time to convince the latter – she was a strapping young girl – that she'd have to scrub and clean like the rest of us. Those Dutchwomen married to Britishers felt Mrs Tjarda should have very special privileges, including the bath shed kept for her own use at special times, to show the Japanese that they at least honoured her. I couldn't help thinking that the Japanese were more likely to respect her if they saw that despite the filthy work she kept her dignity.

Another internee brought in late was Lili Kraus, the famous Hungarian pianist. After fifteen months we were starved of beauty in any form, and some of us asked Mrs Tjarda to try to get the Japanese to agree to our having a concert, but she refused. In fact, she had apparently heard that her husband was one of those taken to Japan which may have decided her it was better to keep out of it. Eventually permission was given.

It was near Christmas, 1943, and though most of us tried not to think of it, we were all feeling pretty miserable and ill too. The concert was given in the huge room we used as a food-serving hall. It had walls with barred windows high up, and the rafters were hung with cobwebs and filth, which we could not reach to clean.

An old upright piano was brought in for Lili, and all who could leave their children and were well enough came and squatted on the broken tiled floor. Outside it was cold and wet, but inside we soon began to steam and get warm as we crouched close together in the gloom. Lili came in and sat at the piano, which was lit with two guttering candles which threw eerie shadows over the huge barnlike building. Her black hair hung, as usual, in thick plaits over her shoulders, and she looked more gypsy-like than usual. She played, I don't remember what, and there was complete silence. When at last she came to an end, it being time for us to be shut in for the night, we got up and walked silently away, many women crying bitterly.

After Christmas the second block of the prison was cleared to receive the hundreds of international refugees who were put with us. We were sorry in many ways when they arrived, as since they had stayed free they did not realize that we had learned in a very hard school to share what we had. One or two, particularly

Yugoslavian, were generous and gave clothes and more than they could well spare themselves, but some of the newcomers behaved abominably. Since I had many Jewish friends, I was particularly upset at the behaviour of some of the wealthier Jewish women who came in.

When the second block was filled, in some ways the camp did brighten – not only because we got much needed clothes, as we hated to have to go around in rags or badly patched things – but because we also had radio news. It was impossible to manage to appear tidy when tiled floors had to be scrubbed, lavatories and drains cleaned out, often in our only pair of shorts or a skirt, and with our bare hands. Sweat and hard work had worn our clothes to rags.

We understood the British were to be moved to another camp in January, 1944, but unfortunately by that time several of the women had typhoid fever, and were removed to an Indonesian hospital in Batavia. There were also cases of diphtheria in the prison, and as the rain poured down day after day, the situation became unbearable.

Every morning at eight the Japanese and native staff of the prison assembled in the outer courtyard whilst the Japanese flag was hoisted, and sang what we took to be the Japanese National Anthem. As soon as this began, crowds of women came to the doors of the big rooms waiting to be allowed out, as well as some women from the cells, carrying sanitation buckets and pots. This queue, sometimes a hundred deep, pushed into the already overcrowded lavatory.

Those who find 'slopping out' in British prisons

disgusting would have been appalled by the conditions of the women and children in Tanah Tinggi.

Once again we had practically no medical aid, for though some of the Salvation Army women ran the hospital, we very seldom saw a doctor, and serious cases were sent either to Tangarang to an Indonesian doctor or, if nearly dying, to the hospital in Batavia. Some of the Salvation Army sisters were wonderful, especially those who had given their lives to work in Javanese villages. Two such women, one of whom had worked in a leper colony and the other with Indonesian beggars, ran a dispensary in the row of cells for which I was later responsible. I had an enormous respect and admiration for those two women who worked month after month, when they were too ill to stand up properly themselves, and sometimes dealt with up to a hundred patients a day.

One mother who came into the camp with her three children much later than us – she was Indonesian – was expecting a baby. There was no doctor, so Sister Digby, one of the dispensers, had to deal with it, with the help of other members of the Salvation Army. The woman had her baby on the plank bed in her cell, with women and children lying three or four per cell on each side of her. I shall never forget little Digby's face when she came across the compound to say that the baby had arrived safely – fortunately at night when some of the internees slept – and that it was the two thousandth baby she had delivered!

The collection of women interned together at that time was a truly curious one. An Indonesian married to a Britisher was interned with five children of her own, plus two of her gardener's children who happened to be playing in the garden when she was picked up. They were forced to stay with us throughout internment. Perhaps because of the dreadful conditions outside it was just as well, though the foster mother was very unkind to them.

Considering the mixture of nationalities, we got on well enough in the camp. It was certainly evident that bad or good behaviour had nothing to do with skin colour, race or religion. Nevertheless, there were a few Englishwomen who, I am sorry to say, even after a year's internment, were rude to girls of mixed birth from Singapore and elsewhere. It made me very angry.

If anything good can come from the horror of war, I hope one thing at least will be clear. The accident of birth is a very chancy thing, and though we may be thankful for the conditions of our upbringing, it little behoves us to sneer at others because of their country or colour. How I wish that all British people were reminded on leaving home that they go as representatives of their country, and as such will be judged.

8

Waiting to Move

Illness amongst the original internees increased as we waited to hear when we were to be moved, and depression and misery were rife.

Because of the new international refugees, we were warned that the *Kempei* were coming to search both blocks, and matters were made worse when the internationals got the wind up and pushed thousands of guilder notes down the sanitation drains. This money washed out through the camp, and so obviously the Japanese found it, which made them keener than ever for a search.

Like most prisons in the world before inspection, all had to appear abnormally clean and tidy. However, then the inspections were postponed from hour to hour, and mostly took place about three o'clock in the afternoon. Throughout the morning and afternoon each internee had to stand in her place in cell or large room at a moment's notice. Furthermore, all the floors, especially the long tiled corridors, had to be spotlessly clean. If it rained, as it all too frequently did, children had to be rounded up and the corridor rewiped at each false alarm, and by mid-afternoon tempers ran high.

It was at such times that the rows between women – mostly over children or their behaviour – flared up, and when I was in charge of a row of cells I was thankful when an inspection day ended peacefully.

When the *Kempei* came to the prison at the end of

January, 1944, all internees were told to stand down in the compound, leaving all cases and luggage open for inspection. I had very little myself, but it was amazing how the possession of some small forbidden object could cause panic.

I remember one woman rushing to me to ask me to keep a stamp – a Dutch 50-cent one – for her. We had been warned we would be punished if found with anything national, and the stamp had the Dutch Queen's head on it! Of course such things sound ridiculous now, but show under what fear many of the internees lived. By that time we were all thankful when search or inspection ended without punishment, for we had by then lost much of our former cocky manner.

On the eve of one search, when Deborah and I were sitting outside her cell, Ferne asleep inside, with our legs dangling in the gutter, Angelina, the Yugoslav, came leaping by in great agitation. She had hidden some thousands of guilders in the bamboo pole used on the great washing rack outside her cell. Many people had hung their washing when the inspection ended, and she could not find her pole!

We all searched fruitlessly, but it had obviously been lost or stolen. Rather unkindly, the whole thing struck us as decidedly comic, for though we realized fully how useful the money would be later, it was so typical of Angelina.

A curious situation arose subsequently over money. Although technically all the internees had handed over their money the previous year, whenever the food position was particularly bad, the Japanese allowed those who had money to pool it to buy extra food for the camp, and this curious arrangement persisted right up to the end of the war! Had it not been for the savings of these women, many fewer of us would have survived.

Amongst the new internees was a young Jewish girl who had hoped to go with her parents to have her voice further trained in America. She was about the same age as the young Deanna Durbin, an American popular singer of the time, and much like her, and she certainly had a most beautiful voice.

One night she and her mother were given permission to come from the Jewish block and stay the night in the fish market. It was a dark, rainy night, causing shadows from the huge trees which dripped dolefully in the centre of the compound. By the faint light from each cell, and the slightly brighter one which shone through the great barred door of the fish market, a strange sight was to be seen.

In every cell door appeared a pale face, very often a thin arm hung through the bars, and in the large rooms a dim, white-faced crowd gathered by the barred doors. Everyone was listening. From the shadowy crowd near the door, a young girl with wavy hair stepped to the grille, and her lovely voice carried right over the prison compound. For once the children were quiet, and even the wardresses stopped their usual chatter.

The girl – I no longer remember her name – first sang 'The Lights of Home', and though for many people there it had no real significance, and possibly was not even understood, the effect was overpowering, and it was more than we could bear. Luckily she turned to lighter songs, and we all ended the evening joining her in 'It's a long way to Tipperary', the ever-popular favourite.

Unfortunately, such treats were rare, and our situation became grave when we were told that as we had 'technically' moved in January, we could have no sugar, soap or other necessities brought in. This was not the first, nor the last, time that we were to be without soap. Even when we did get it, it was usually prison-made by the convicts and never hardened, so however careful we were it quickly melted away.

There was nothing we could do about it, and at least had to be thankful for a fairly adequate water supply, which many camps had not.

My one bright spot was looking after young Ferne, who was growing well, despite the horrible conditions under which she was being brought up. She was a jolly youngster of one-and-a-half, and I had the greatest fun helping her mother with her washing, feeding and games. Deborah by this time was living mainly on rolled cigarettes, pseudo-coffee and brown sugar, when we could get them.

The food was bad, consisting of a mug of coffee-water and a plate of grey rice porridge, which usually looked as if it had been scraped from a very dirty kitchen floor before we got it, for breakfast. At one o'clock we lined up by the 'dining room' and room by room passed the servers with our tin plates, each room or block of cells moving up one place in the queue each day. We took turns working as servers, which also meant cleaning out the dining room, and dividing out the food. This latter was a thankless and rather tricky job, when about seven hundred people had to be fed, with portions which varied from day to day – according to how much the criminals in the prison kitchen managed to pinch.

For the midday meal we each had a ladle of rice and a tin mug of stringy vegetables, which most of us drank as soup, hoping that it contained lots of iron – it certainly didn't have much vegetable. Once a week we got a better meal of meat or a little fish with the rice, and quite a lot of vegetables in various forms. We also got peanuts, and half a hard-boiled duck's egg. This meal was even more of a nightmare to deal out than the usual miserable portion, as everyone watched hungrily each luscious grain.

In the evening at five o'clock we were given another plate of horrible rice porridge, into which we put a little lump of 'goela Java', a sort of solidified molasses, or some peanut butter, if we had it.

By March all these delights were finished, and the children lay on their pallets weak from lack of sugar and other food. Then at last it was sent in, kilos and kilos of solid brown sugar which in the old days we should never have dreamed of eating until it had been boiled and filtered.

Things were different now, and we broke off chunks and gobbled it up, not minding the dead flies, bits of wood or even lizards' tails embedded in it. 'Goela Java' is very moreish stuff, and never more so than on that occasion, when little children ran out of their cells, their mouths and hands sticky from the sugar, and laughed and played in the compound once again. Alas, it is also very laxative, and the next night we all suffered the tortures of the damned for our day's enjoyment.

At the end of March, 1944, we were actually told to be ready to move to a fresh camp, and I was worried not only over Deborah's condition, but also because

Emmy was very thin and weak with a bad cough, and Elvira, who had been sent away to Batavia with bad blood-poisoning in her arm, had not returned. I was much afraid that the horrible conditions in the hospital, and the fact that she had to wear Indonesian clothes and suffer many indignities, might be too much for her. Luckily she had the pluck to stick it all, and joined us again later.

The day of the trek we put all our mattress rolls in one room, to be taken by freight car, and formed into a line about two o'clock in the afternoon to walk the two kilometres to our new home. I had made a sling from a scarf, such as the Indonesians use, to carry Ferne on my hip, whilst Deborah and I carried such luggage as we had on a bamboo pole between us. She was in no state for such a walk, for she should have had an operation some time previously, and was often in great pain though she hid it very bravely. Though she was terribly thin, her legs were dreadfully swollen, but when I begged her to go on the freight car which was to take a few serious cases from the hospital, she refused.

Despite two searches of the prison by the Secret Police, who had taken away watches, wedding rings and money amongst other things, I had always managed to keep my tiny blue leather case, which contained my last sewing equipment, my passport and a few photographs. At the last moment, I found I could not carry everything, so pushed the little blue case into my mattress roll, under the interested eye of one of the wardresses, who had previously told me how much she admired it. I was worried, but there was nothing else I could do as I certainly couldn't carry it. I took out my passport, the broken scissors and two photos of the children and Charles as a precaution.

At about two-thirty we moved out of the prison – a most pitiable collection of humanity, covered with ulcers on arms and legs on which the flies settled, and laden with bits of luggage, tins, buckets and bags, for by this time we had learned to hang on like grim death to any nail, tin or bit of string. I wore Charles's old tweed jacket despite the heat, so that as usual I became a walking cupboard.

The few Indonesians who were out in the heat of the day turned their heads away in embarrassment as, nagged unceasingly by the Japanese guards, we dragged our way along the hot dusty road, wondering what our new camp was to hold for us.

9

Tangarang Reformatory

As we staggered through a high gateway into the new prison, we saw faces peering at us from behind barbed wire in the compound on our right. Later we heard that these were the women and children from the Dutch camps in Soerabaja who had been moved away because of the Allied bombing. For once this was not a rumour, for the women had seen something of it through the shutters of the train.

The British group were ordered through to a separate compound, and divided out into the rooms which surrounded it, then locked in. The one which Deborah and I found ourselves in housed seventy-eight women and children. The floor was broken cement and mud, and along each of the filthy walls ran wooden platforms, the lower about two feet from the ground. An upper shelf had been added, with a steep wooden ladder leading up to it, about three feet above the lower platform, and these double-decker platforms ran down each side of the long room.

When we were first herded in, the decks had a curious shimmering appearance, which effect was produced by the thousands of bugs which covered the boards, and poured into the cracks as we approached.

Since there was no rail along the upper platforms, we decided that mothers with small children would have to use the lower ones, though they were hopelessly dark and airless. After a month in this dreadful place Deborah, like other mothers, had hard lumps on her knuckles and knees through crawling to the back of her sleeping-place – it was impossible even to sit upright on a mattress on the under-deck. The buildings had originally been a reformatory, but had been used for Dutch troops before we arrived. As was often the case, it was left in a very dirty condition, and the bugs were much worse than in any women's camp at that time.

After being locked in our rooms for some hours, we were at last allowed out to the lavatories. I went to collect our mattresses, only to find my little blue case had been stolen. There was of course nothing I could do about it, for every camp we left meant the loss of our possessions one by one, but I was furious.

When we put our mattresses down for the night, one yard per person, Deborah managed to fix a small mosquito net over Ferne's corner, and then a second piece of net over that, and in this way she was kept partially free from the dreadful ravages of the mosquitoes and bugs, which poured out of the cracks at night. The smell of the squashed ones was disgusting, and we were all of us streaked with blood from the bites in the morning, after a miserable night.

In the second block of the reformatory there was a cooking shed, much the same as at Lengkong, only larger. On the night we arrived we were served a meal cooked and prepared by women and boys from the Soerabaja blocks. These big boys of anything up to eighteen years were a great help in the camp, and were well disciplined in one building by a Mrs Wichers, formerly in charge of the Scouts in Soerabaja. She was strict but just, and the lads behaved very differently from some of those we were to meet later when we were next moved to the huge Tjideng camp in Batavia.

The Dutch Soerabaja camp, which included a Jewish group, had been a good one. Most of the women and children were only interned in late 1943, and even then they were only shut in at night, being allowed to go out shopping and visiting during daylight until shortly before their journey to West Java. The tales some of them had to tell of chickens, milk, eggs, cheese and cream, which until recently they had enjoyed, made our mouths water.

They had brought an enormous amount of luggage with them – though as women who had been living in comfortable quarters and only recently been forced to part with some of their possessions – they appeared to feel badly done by. For the first few weeks they refused to eat the maize porridge which in Tangarang was our staple diet. We had this maize coarsely ground twice a day in place of our former rice diet – the Indonesians in East Java eat maize, unlike the Soendanese in West Java – and it had the most ghastly effect on those of us already weak with dysentery. The first plateful was served after the morning roll-call, sometimes with a bit of brown sugar added, and a can of weak tea. At one o'clock we lined up again and each room got a bucket of maize, a zinc bath of watery vegetable soup, and occasionally some dried fish, or half a duck's egg. We also got, and highly prized, *sambel* made from chillis and other spices, because of its high vitamin content. After a time we could eat red chillis raw with our maize, but only the most asbestos-mouthed could manage to eat a green one.

The children in the British block were starving by

this time, and went gladly each day to the refuse bins in the Dutch block to pick out what porridge they could find, not to mention remains of cheese, sugar, biscuits, bread, etc., which had been thrown away in the bins.

I was head of my room by this time, and had many rude things to hear about the way the British children went 'grubbing' for refuse when I attended the daily meeting of *kapalas* (heads) in the office. Luckily our camp leader, Mrs Vrede, was fair and kindly, and she certainly earned her name, which means 'Peace', and poured oil on many troubled waters. We were also helped with desperately needed clothes by our more fortunate neighbours, who were most generous. Unfortunately I must confess that some of the better-provided Britishers grabbed what they could get, and feelings often ran high.

It was often difficult for the Dutchwomen to realize that we had been interned under very bad conditions for one and a half years, and that most of us started internment with practically nothing, whilst they had, in many cases, been interned in European houses with comparative plenty in the way of space, furniture, clothing and so on.

Furthermore, there was far too much recrimination about the war. A great many Dutch had been pro-German before the invasion of Holland in 1940, and had expected – as one of their Cabinet Ministers wrote – to remain neutral and make a hundred per cent profit as they had done in the First World War. I remember staying in Buitenzorg with the wife of a high Dutch official before the invasion, and she told me scornfully that her brother was in the Dutch Army on the frontier and found the Germans absolutely charming, and that they would never dream of invading Holland!

Alas, Germany did invade, and the feelings of the Dutch turned in most cases to hate, especially as they had fed so many German children during the blockade of Germany after the First World War, and felt these children had turned against them after their great kindness. Up to the time of the German invasion of Dutch territory, Holland was determined to maintain strict neutrality, so many Dutch people in the Indies were shocked, and it is a fact that in places in Sumatra the officials were uncertain for a time whether it was the British or the Germans who were to be interned!

Consequently, the British were looked on as trouble-makers. The fall of Singapore had been a bitter blow to our prestige, not only for its strategic position, but also because Dutch pilots and planes had flown from Java to help resist the Japanese invasion, and this helped to weaken the Dutch resistance in Java, never very strong in the first place. Because of these circumstances, the British and Dutch kept largely to their own blocks, though it was very difficult to avoid trouble.

Many British women of mixed blood had been helping in the kitchens from the beginning because they understood how to make the best of the local foods provided by the Japanese. One day, however, things came to a head in Tangarang.

Several of us had been stamping maize, which had been brought unmilled into the camp as the millers had been on strike, or for some other reason been unable to grind the meal. As I can't imagine any miller going on strike with a Japanese standing over him with a bayonet, I dare say it was a new form of punishment devised for our benefit. Be that as it may, the maize had to be stamped, which meant putting the coarse grain in a hollow wooden drum, and crushing it with a heavy wooden stamper, just as one saw Indonesians doing in the *kampongs* of Java.

A squad of us had been doing this till we were quite exhausted, and we suggested that the much stronger young Dutch lads and girls might take a turn. We were sharply told that as most of our people appeared to be near-native, and they understood the procedure, they should get on with it. Of course, there was trouble, and I'm glad to say that later the Soerabaja block took on all the heavy work, for by then most of us were too sick to be able to do much, and they helped us considerably.

More trouble began when the Jewish group from Soerabaja were put in two rooms beside the open kitchen. After a time the inmates had to be locked in their rooms when the kitchen was being cleaned during the afternoon, to stop thieving. Even the Japanese eventually found the occupants of these rooms too much to cope with, and the group were locked up when there was an inspection by a Japanese and we had to stand out on the big cement parade ground. Even then, the young Jewish boys would get up on the higher platforms in their rooms and jeer and shout throughout the inspection.

The first of these Jewish rooms was next door to ours, and nights were made extra hideous by screams and yells as some of the inmates fought, or were caught thieving. One day I was called along because one of the boys had thrown some slops from a chamber pot over the corridor and refused to clear it up. The mother was afraid of trouble, and came to me, saying, 'You come,

Mrs. My boy, he no good. They tell you make him clean floor.'

I gathered that I had got a strict reputation from some of the Lengkong mothers, which seemed a bit hard as the children had loved their school, and had even, together with some help from mothers, embroidered all their names on a handkerchief for me, with a circular message, 'In remembrance of Happy School Days in Camp!' Since I believed children preferred some sort of discipline, which gave them a sense of security, we all got along fine with settled lessons, drill and games at Lengkong. At least it was something which remained sure from day to day in a rocking world.

After some weeks in Tangarang I started English lessons at Mrs Wichers's suggestion for three classes of Dutch boys, and thoroughly enjoyed this new work. The Lengkong children had already been taken over in Tanah Tinggi by a quaint old German-American from the Salvation Army, since I had little time after being put in charge of the women and children's block of cells.

I was therefore glad to teach in Tangarang, and used a geography book and a copy of Marshall's *Our Island Story*, lent me by one of the women.

Formerly I had been amused, and sometimes angered, by the biased way history was taught in Britain and other countries. It was interesting to hear comments about former battles with the Dutch from my pupils! The senior class – boys of from fifteen to seventeen – were most interested in English customs and etiquette, and were full of eager questions. They also thirsted for knowledge of our grammar, and there I found myself in very deep water but managed to struggle through. I believe the boys enjoyed the lessons as much as I did.

One boy did me a very good turn indeed, for when working in a sort of repair shop left behind by the soldiers, he found a bucket which leaked and had been thrown away. Filling the bottom with coarse black 'hair' from the coconut palm, he added a new wooden bottom, and presented me with a beautiful bucket which lasted for the rest of internment. I was tremendously grateful, for until then I had been obliged to borrow one from Elvira which was getting badly worn, and I did not know how to replace it.

In Tangarang we got our water from two taps in the main compound, and it was necessary to filter it through a bit of rag to get rid of the larger worms, with which the water seethed. We were not supposed to drink it, but we were over two thousand people in a reformatory meant for six hundred. With the cooking drums allowed, it was quite impossible to boil enough drinking water as well as cook food.

We again had trouble over the sanitary conditions, as each block had only one lavatory with eight 'stalls' for about four hundred people. Through an iron gate leading to the parade ground, a long line of latrines had been built for the soldiers, but at night this door was locked and a Japanese guard stood on duty there, so it was impossible to get out. After some days on the maize diet even those of the British who till then had not suffered too badly from dysentery were now in a shocking state. Many could not manage to stagger the length of the long corridors to the lavatory, which in any case was quickly blocked up at night, so that the floor became a swimming cesspool. In the daytime the flies made matters worse, and sickness increased alarmingly.

When the British came to Tangarang, the heads of each room in our block held a meeting to decide what should be done about a hospital, for though the Salvation Army had done their best in Tanah Tinggi, some of us felt it had not been very satisfactory. After some argument it was decided it should be left to the nuns from the big Catholic hospital in Soerabaja – one of the best in Java – since they were now interned with us. They took over, and certainly did their best in shocking circumstances, until all nuns were later concentrated in one Java camp.

In Tangarang we were for the first time entirely under the Japanese, and the tighter discipline was immediately noticeable.

A day or two after arrival, we were told to assemble on the big parade ground at the back of the reformatory, except those who were really sick. Deborah, luckily, was able to stay in our room with Ferne, though it was always risky as the Japanese inspected each barracks to see who stayed in, and it was a toss-up whether it was worse standing in the sun or staying in a room.

About eleven-thirty, the head of all Java camps came, preceded by a smart Japanese officer, who at once spotted a woman with covered head, and shouted at her. The Commandant made his speech – the stock one about our being in protective custody. We didn't believe it then, but looking back I think it could well have been true, as the Indonesians made it plain they were determined to win their country its independence.

On the parade ground the officer saw a woman take

a drink of water. He strode from the platform, called
the woman out, and knocked her over the head. After
which the official party left, and we were told to stand
where we were, for many hours, as punishment.

We were later to learn much of this officer, by name
Sonè, for when we got to Tjideng camp he was in
charge, and his name became a byword for cruelty.

The leader of the British block at this time was a
part-Chinese girl from Singapore, Dulcie Nicholas, and
she certainly seemed to understand the mentality and
worked better with the Japanese than anyone else,
perhaps due to the fact that she also, like the Japanese
Commandant and the nuns who ran the hospital, was
a Catholic. Possibly also, with her Chinese education
she could get closer to Japanese thinking.

In any case, without being too friendly with the
Japanese, Dulcie did a lot of good work for the camp,
for which many people, even though they did not like
her, were grateful.

10
Orang Miskin – the Beggars

Once the work had been allotted in the reformatory, we settled down, and it was really amazing to see how soon the women and children adapted themselves to the new conditions. We had arrived at Tangarang during the rainy season, but by May, 1944, the fine weather had set in and the nights were cool.

Each room had a head and a deputy head, and in our room I had a Swiss woman to help me who, like Emmy, was a very good worker and scrupulously clean. Unfortunately Mrs Simington was greedy, and so the apportioning of food or clothes had to be carefully watched, for it was such women who got us a bad reputation with the Dutch blocks by taking things when they did not urgently need them, to the detriment of the women and children who were in rags.

I found it increasingly hard to go to the clothes allocation shed to ask for something badly needed by some woman, and hear that our room had already taken more than enough. However, apart from this serious fault, Mrs Simington was both practical and very hard-working, and we had need of such women. Though many of the seventy-eight in our room were sick, the room still had to be cleaned every day, and the wide tiled corridor outside washed each morning. We also had to send two women daily to work with a squad who cleaned the filthy lavatory and washrooms, and others to help in the kitchen cleaning vegetables and preparing the maize, and so on. Others had to go in the afternoon to help clean up the kitchen, clean out the big drums and *wadjangs*, wash the floors, and other work. After some weeks the Soerabaja block took over all cooking and stoking of fires, which was very heavy work, and this helped the British women a lot.

At about half-past twelve after the daily meeting of all room orderlies in the office, the heads of each room and four or five helpers went to fetch the buckets of food from the kitchen, which was then served to the file of people waiting on the verandah outside each room. We divided our room into groups, so that the line changed from week to week, and so far as possible everyone got a fair share. If, in dealing out food, there was a little left over, one group came again for more and these groups also, of course, came in rotation.

After the midday meal, the pails and buckets were washed and most people tried to get a short rest, despite the noise of all the children. Many of us got up before first light in order to get to the taps and wash our few ragged clothes before the rush began, so we were more than ready to lie down by two o'clock.

Some people played bridge, or did lessons, and two or three afternoons a week I was teaching, but unfortunately at this time I had to end my French lessons with Madame Caly, partly because she was getting very tired but also because my time was rather limited.

One great relaxation in Tangarang for me was to listen to Lili Kraus, who of course had come with us, practising each morning in a shed off the parade ground. I always tried to get through my work so that I could go and sit near the shed to listen to her for a short while. It was forbidden by the Japanese, but with a little care was quite possible, and well worth the risk.

On two moonlight evenings Lili was again allowed to give concerts in Tangarang, and the sight of the motionless crowd squatting on the ground was quite unforgettable. I do not believe she, or any other great artist who gave concerts in internment camps, will ever have more appreciative audiences or give so much pleasure.

Morning and evening the whole camp had to line up in twos along the corridors for inspection, and each leader called her group to attention and gave the number of sick and healthy in her room. These totals had to be given to Mrs Vrede early each morning, so that she could give the totals to the Japanese who came round with her. The numbers altered constantly, and there was always trouble with the counting. This was the first camp in which we had twice daily roll-call.

As the Japanese and the camp head reached each block, we were called to attention in Japanese, then as he approached, each room was given the orders: *kioskè* (attention), *kerè* (bow), *norè* (stand upright), *wakerè* (stand at ease). These are phonetic spellings, as I never learned Japanese, but we got to know the sounds well enough over the years!

The second rollcall in the evening took place after our food had been distributed, but before we had time to eat it. It was necessary therefore to cover what one had both from the flies, and also from thieving. Most people were covered with tropical ulcers, and had no rags to use as bandages, so the flies were a terrible scourge.

Ferne was always washed and put to bed before supper, and after rollcall and our meal, Deborah and I smoked a cigarette – if we had any tobacco. Sometimes we were given extra sugar, soap, tobacco and a few other things which were paid for by women who handed in their money for that purpose, but we always had trouble to find paper to use for cigarettes. I had recently finished another play, but had been sorely tempted to smoke the paper.

Lights out was at ten o'clock, and was strictly enforced, but as space per person was so limited – about a 75 cm width, and the bugs vicious despite all our efforts to clean out the cracks with knitting needles – it was almost impossible to sleep. Frequently I sat outside in the compound, and so long as one listened for the guard doing rounds, and did not get caught, it was fairly safe, and was very pleasant – and above all quiet – outside.

Fond as I am of my Dutch friends, and I have many, they do have penetrating voices, and their children often have very bad table-manners, to our way of thinking. That this is not a fallacy could be proved by any traveller who, after staying in the big Hotel des Indes in Batavia, moved on to one of the Singapore hotels. Even Dutch friends who did have well-brought-up children told me that they dreaded the journey to Holland on a Dutch boat, despite the wonderful accommodation, because the effect of the other children's bad manners would be terrible.

In the camps, very few people retained good manners, and the speed with which some degenerated into little more than animals was horrifying. Thieving, lying, telling tales to curry favour with guards or staff went on all the time. As far as I could see, the old saying that trouble brought out the best in one was very

–

much a half-truth. The good people in camp got better, but the bad ones got far, far worse.

One of the necessary, but unpleasant, tasks in Tangarang was cleaning the fish. Not that we grumbled when there was fish to eat, but the Japanese always seemed to deliver it late in the evening, and volunteers had to go from each room to help clean it. Even this would not have been so bad, but unfortunately the job seldom finished before two or three in the morning, after which there was a rush for the washrooms where we tried to clean ourselves and our hair of fishscales. Since we were often without soap, it was not easy. The water was icy, and the wind whistled through the shed. At such times, coming from a very hot kitchen I was more than grateful to Gerrit and Ita for the army blanket they'd given me. When I had to try to wash it in my bucket, though, it was not an easy job.

Despite all our washing, the smell of fish stuck to us, and as many of us had only two pairs of threadbare shorts or skirts by this time, it was difficult to keep them even partly clean. Most of us were barefooted, or occasionally had *klompen*, by then.

At the beginning of June rumours began to circulate that the British were once again to be moved, and at the same time we received our first parcels which came from the American Red Cross. Mrs Vrede was willing for them to be divided out in the British block, but this was vetoed, and apart from the few Americans who, with their children, each got a full parcel, the rest of the camp received one or two tins according to the size. The cigarettes were dealt out to those who smoked, and the rest of the camp got chocolate.

To ensure a fair distribution, the tins were given out

by lottery, though even then the head office had a hard job, and there was much grumbling. Women from the Soerabaja group still had tinned food which they had brought into Tangarang with them, and used the American gift tins to bribe girls from the British block to do their washing and other duties for them, which caused great resentment.

At length, on 15 June, we were told to be ready to leave camp, and thankfully packed our mattresses and last small belongings once more.

In the early hours of the morning we were on the move, this time in a fairly comfortable train, and taken to the big Dutch internment camp at Tjideng, which was in the middle of Batavia. We were even given sweets and biscuits as a last present from Tangarang, which came as a delightful surprise.

Until a few months previously, Tjideng camp had been on two sides of a large canal, and the occupants allowed to move freely in and out during the day, as the Soerabaja Dutch had also done. In April, after the Soerabaja bombing, the camp was made smaller, and the Dutchwomen were told to hand in their money. They were also stopped leaving the camp, and put on rations. At this time there were about three thousand women and children, as well as some boys and old men, in Tjideng, and they lived in what had been small residential bungalows. I heard part of the quarter had been the red-light district of Batavia, so no doubt the Japanese found it amusing to use such quarters.

After the war when Emmy Starkey had an article published in a South African paper, *Outspan*, this is what she wrote:

Then came another move. The British-American group had to pack up again, and was taken to Batavia, to be interned in a Dutch camp, Tjideng. We were a sorry sight, enfeebled by lack of food and medicines, clothes patched and worn, many with bare feet. During the two years we had been interned we had never been allowed to buy clothes, or to communicate with friends and have some sent in. What had been decent clothes at first were now rags, hardly clean, because soap was unobtainable. Most of us looked like walking skeletons, thin and haggard, unable even to carry our meagre belongings without the help of the stronger ones.

This was an accurate picture of our group, and as we lined up and waited in the hot sun, our luggage was searched and any papers – mostly recipes which women wrote to stem their ever-increasing hunger – were taken away and torn up. I also lost the two plays I had written and a precious notebook.

At last we were told to move through the big doors and high bamboo stockade into the camp, and as we divided into the bungalows allocated to us, we thankfully dropped down on the floor. Dutch friends from the camp hurried to us with tears in their eyes, bringing clothes, towels, soap, and we received the most wonderful welcome.

Sonè, the Japanese head of the camp, had told the Dutch that the *orang miskin* (beggars) were coming, and that we were to be helped.

It needed no such reminder from a Japanese to prompt our friends to hurry to help in every way, so that for the first weeks we thought we were in heaven, with wonderful food and no work to do.

Although conditions before long became even more appalling in Tjideng than in other camps, we were eternally grateful for the help and welcome shown to us when we first arrived.

11
Tjideng Camp, Batavia

By the time the British were brought to Tjideng the camp was shut off by high double stockades, and had a large main street with smaller streets leading off, and yet smaller roads lying parallel. The Dutch then were living in bungalows, with a fair amount of furniture, about seven people in each.

When we were brought in from Tangarang we were divided up into large bungalows near the main gates, opposite a hospital, and were greatly helped by Dr Rijkebusch, a Dutch woman practitioner, who came daily to examine us, and give what treatment was possible. She did everything she could for us, and many of the British owed their lives to her. After the war I heard she had been ostracized by the Dutch in Batavia for working with the Japanese. If true, I can only say she worked unceasingly as a doctor for all who needed medical care.

At that time the hospital was large, and staffed by volunteer nurses and doctors, some of them male. We also had two of the finest surgeons in the camp with us, famous in Batavia before the war, who did wonderful work in extremely difficult circumstances.

As well as doctors and specialists, there were dentists, and this was a blessing for many of our group who were already suffering from broken and unfilled teeth. Once in Bandoeng I had been allowed to visit the Indonesian dentist. When I asked him to fill the cavity with a temporary stopping so that it could be done later by my own dentist, he roared with laughter and said he thought he'd better put in a very permanent one, which he did. Perhaps just as well, as that was December, 1942, and it appeared I had been slightly optimistic!

By the time we reached Tjideng in June, 1944, many internees had such trouble with teeth breaking because of insufficient and starchy food that, despite chalk and vitamins, it was too late to help them. Their teeth broke off bit by bit, only the stumps remaining at the end of internment.

For the first weeks our meals were brought to us and served by Dutch volunteers, and they gave us the best they had, including meat and fat which we had not seen for months. Also fruit and vegetables, so that most of us felt very much better after a few weeks. For others, alas, it was already too late, and a number of young children and some adults died shortly after we moved, the richer food sometimes being too much for them.

Before this there had been no deaths in our original Bandoeng group, and we had tried to keep together whenever possible, though this was not easy because of all the work and the fact that we met old, or made new, friends in each camp. One thing the British learned, and that was the necessity in the peculiar circumstances in which we were forced to live to pool all food, and cook for the whole house or camp, so that the best could be made of the small amount given us.

Most of the Dutch internees at this period – and for some time afterwards – continued to cook individually, so that in one bungalow there would be four or five people who cooked in different rooms or the garden, on little charcoal stoves. Whilst some had plenty of tinned foods to add to meals, others had nothing.

Because we had no furniture and little luggage, the British were immediately put forty or more per bungalow. Nevertheless it was paradise compared with anything we had recently been used to, and as we gradually collected a few bits of furniture which the Dutch threw out into their gardens as they became more crowded themselves, we felt we were in clover.

Deborah, Ferne and I shared a room with a Mrs Ribiera and her daughters, who had come via Singapore from Sarawak. Though we still slept on the floor, we were able to fix mosquito nets, and keep the tiles clean. The mosquitoes were simply ferocious, probably because the old wells at the back of the bungalows had not been cleaned out since the invasion, and were filled with every sort of rubbish. Internees who had not got netting either had to suffocate under a blanket in the sweltering night, or be severely bitten so that they looked like a bad case of measles the following morning: the danger of malaria was also greatly increased.

There was a large vegetable market in Tjideng, and a general 'store' from which rations for each bungalow had to be collected weekly. Some meat still came in, though naturally it decreased in quantity and quality as the size of the camp increased. Those who were ill were able to get an 'attest' from a doctor allowing them extra meat, dried and fresh vegetables, and occasionally eggs. Unfortunately those who were not really ill sometimes cheated the doctors, to the disadvantage of the desperately sick.

Morning and evening all internees except the sick and those on duty at the hospital attended rollcall in the long main street, and were counted block by block. All went well as long as Sonè – or the officers who aped him – was in a good mood, but if he was drunk, or, worse still, unable to get drink, his temper was filthy and we could expect shouting, kicking and beating if anyone annoyed him.

At first the camp seemed wonderful after all we had been through, but as Sonè's temper gradually became worse, a feeling of terror descended on Tjideng, and as punishment followed punishment people became afraid, and suspicious even of members in their own house, whilst rumours flew round with ever-increasing speed.

When we had been some weeks in the bungalows near the main gate, we were told that we must move, as other women were coming in, and we were then allotted ten much smaller bungalows in one of the small side streets. Those on the other side of the street were occupied by Dutchwomen, and it was not long before there was trouble over the disposal of sewage.

At the end of the little street was a long field which had probably been used as a playing field by the surrounding houses before the war. At the end nearest to our street were six sheds containing lavatories with an open cesspool behind, covered in wire. This cesspool was by then bubbling over, and covered with flies. We considered that it should be cleaned out, but the women opposite told us that as they never used the sheds, they would not help. Nevertheless, many of them continued to empty chamber pots into the open drain which ran along the row of houses to the lavatories.

The back walls of our ten bungalows, because they lay next to the bamboo stockade, had been broken by the Japanese, so that what had been the servants' lavatory now had a wall through it, with a stockade beyond. We therefore had only one lavatory per house of forty people. Obviously this was inadequate owing to dysentery, and we were forced to make use of the filthy sheds down the road.

At last we decided to send two helpers from each house, plus a squad of Dutch boys who were still in Tjideng, to clean out the sewage. After an hour only three women and two boys were left hauling the filth in old tin cans attached to bamboo poles, until the pool was empty.

Covered with ulcers – some as large as a fist – on which the flies swarmed, and with little soap and no disinfectant to try to get clean, we could not get the awful smell off ourselves or our clothes.

Another source of trouble between the Dutch and British came when the boys were removed to another camp, and young girls took over much of their work, including removal of furniture and heavy lifting, washing the old men who were unable to look after themselves, and other jobs. It was difficult for us to spare girls for the squads as we had so many sick ourselves, but I felt it was the older women who should unload the rice lorries and do other heavy work, in the hope that the young ones one day might be out of camp and able to marry and have children.

When we moved into the new row of bungalows, a large proportion of our houses were British-Indian or part Soendanese and Deborah and I were thankful to be with them. They were nearly all kind and easy to get on with, and understood far better than we did then how to cook the rice, vegetables and spices we received weekly, and made the most delicious dishes from the rations we received. Most important of all, I knew I could rely on them absolutely to look after Deborah and Ferne when I had to be out on other jobs. By this time Deborah was very ill, and could eat very little.

I tried to persuade her to go into hospital, but she steadfastly refused, and in the end I had to agree that she was probably right. When I spoke to one of the doctors about getting extra food for her, I was told that as far as they were concerned, she was dead. She had a raging fever much of the time, and although she was as thin as a rake, her face and legs were painfully swollen, and since she refused to go into hospital they could do no more.

There were times when I was furiously angry with Deborah because she was so stubborn, and sometimes it made things very difficult, but I can see now that she was so desperately ill that nothing but will power brought her through the war, and no hospital treatment could have done more for her at that time. Moreover, she had a horror of being parted from Ferne, and in this I believe she was right. Though I had part charge of Ferne, we never knew when we should be moved or parted from one another, and in fact some months later I was sent to a work camp, and Deborah and Ferne were forced to remain in Tjideng till the end of the war.

During our first months many of our group had to go into the hospital, and although some did die, the death roll was not nearly so heavy as it was to become in later months, when six or eight deaths a day became usual.

Ever since we had left Lengkong, I had always kept contact with 'young' Mrs Raymond – so called to distinguish her from her sister-in-law, 'old' Mrs Raymond, who was also with us from the beginning with her nine daughters. Young Mrs Raymond had three children, and I taught the two older ones and had been particularly fond of Sarah, who was seven. This was because my youngest daughter Sarah, who had died, would have been the same age.

Little Helene, the youngest, who was only a few months old when the family came into Lengkong, had often been ill before. Sadly, the change to Tjideng food was to prove too much for her, and this little Jewish baby died.

As soon as I could I went along to see the distracted mother, knowing she had loved Helene the most dearly of all her children. I found her in a tiny room, weeping bitterly, with her dead baby lying on a little table, covered with flowers. Helene looked like a tiny waxen doll, and I found it impossible to believe she was dead.

The mother's lamentations rose higher and higher, though I tried to calm her so that the two older children should not be too upset. Suddenly Mrs Raymond was silent: her face became radiant and still, as, softly weeping, she murmured: 'If it is your will, God, I give her to you, and hope it may help to end the war soon.' I shall never forget her face as she spoke.

Such moments were all too rare, for it seemed as though most of the women who professed to be Christian and had attended church regularly in peacetime were lost without clergy to guide them. It seemed so often the outwardly religious woman who lost faith and needed bolstering up, and this struck me as strange. Of course there were really deeply religious and caring women in the camp – Mrs Noordhoek Hegt was a case in point – but those whom we might have expected to give a mental and moral lead were too often unable to do so.

By the time we did get out of the camps and prisons, some of the behaviour we'd witnessed nauseated us. After the war I was asked by the vicar at my daughters' school whether religion had proved a great help to myself and others, and I was bound to say this had not been the case. Perhaps because I was always sure I should see Charles and the children again it was easier for me, though I have always felt that eventually each one of us is responsible for his life and behaviour. In an age when too many children are brought up without any self-discipline, and have the inaccurate idea that the state provides, we shall only have ourselves to blame if these same children later show lack of initiative and enterprise. It is for us now to see that this does not happen.

All this may seem far from life in camp, but one thing about internment was that it threw us back on to our own resources, and gave us the chance to think over many things which, perhaps, we had neither the time nor the inclination to do whilst we lived our normal lives.

I had to thank a friend of ours who had been interned, like my father, in Germany during the First World War for some sound advice. Before he was picked up by the Japanese in Tjioemboeloeit he told me that if by bad luck I was eventually interned, I should immediately make a plan and set myself daily tasks, however trivial. I followed this plan, and found it helped. One had to accept the situation, too, however much one disliked it, and after that things became easier. It was those women who could not do so, and who struggled futilely against their captors in what was bound to be a losing battle, who eventually gave up the struggle and preferred to die. The important thing was to know what was worth making a row about, and what not, and for the rest, the only thing to do was to have patience, of which we garnered an enormous store, and put on as good a face as possible.

12
Punishment Day

Our treatment in Tjideng had been steadily worsening, and early in September a Dutch woman was caught using an electric iron after stern orders had been given that no electric apparatus was allowed. She and her small daughter were dreadfully beaten by Sonè, and the woman's arm was broken.

By August the food had already been cut down, and the stronger Dutchwomen were beginning to feel the strain badly, partly because with the exception of those who had been severely handled by the Secret Police many of them were coming under really bad conditions for the first time. Also, perhaps, because the Dutch as a race are heavy eaters, and felt the lack of food even more than we did. It was nothing for Dutch friends to lose five or six stone in weight, whereas I knew few Englishwomen who lost more than about three stone.

There had again been changes in the camp, those of mixed blood from the British group being removed to Kramat camp, as were also the Jewish women and children, so that I lost touch with many of my friends and did not see Sybil and Helene Baher and their mother until after the war. I never saw Elvira again, but shall always be grateful for her gentleness and kindness in a life where too many people were inclined to forget the existence of manners. She was very ill before she left Tjideng, but after the war good nursing and rest, and eventually reunion with her husband, helped her to regain health.

The terror of Sonè hung over the camp, and each day brought fresh tales of a doctor, nurse or block leader receiving punishment from him. It was quite useless to argue with a Japanese, and many of the misunderstandings came through lack of knowledge of the language. There were a few women who acted as interpreters, who had either been in Japan previously or learned the language for some reason. Unfortunately they were mostly disliked or distrusted by the other women, and it was impossible to check whether one had been truthfully interpreted or not.

On the morning of 30 September 1944, there had been some misunderstanding and trouble in the main office, and at 2 P.M. the whole camp was ordered to assemble on the main street.

Immediately, women and children poured out of the bungalows, hurried on by frightened block leaders who had already heard Sonè's voice and knew the sort of temper he was in. The doctors, who at once went to protest that their patients could not be moved from the hospital, were beaten and told that all patients must come out, if necessary on stretchers, to join the parade.

As we stood in files on the tarmac road, the sun blazing down, and wondered what had happened, the Japanese officers walked up and down the long rows shouting at us. The patients began to creep out of the hospital, many of the worst cases being carried by volunteers on stretchers and placed in the shade of the few trees lining the wide street.

Jopie de Vries, whose husband Piet had gone back to supervise the work on the Company estates for the

Japanese, was by this time in Tjideng hospital, having had a serious abdominal operation the previous day. She refused to move. The Japanese were quite incalculable, for in her case they let her stay in the hospital, though whether because she defied them, or because her husband was technically working for them, it is hard to say.

In many ways, Jopie was like Gerrit, and showed no fear of the Japanese, and did not care in the least what she said to them. In Gerrit's case it was understandable, since both his son and son-in-law were killed during the short fight for Java, and so he took enormous risks against the Japanese by helping people, and got away with it. Other equally brave men and women were caught and executed, some even in the weeks after the end of hostilities.

When we paraded in the main street, some of our very sick Britishers, including Deborah and little Ferne, had remained in the bungalow. As usual, Japanese orders had been misunderstood, and some block leaders thought that not everyone had to attend the parade. Japanese soldiers went to all the bungalows and roughly ordered out any woman or child found lying there, and sent them to a house by the camp gates for examination and punishment.

Whilst the sick women and children were either in the punishment house, or lined up in front of the hospital, the doctors once more protested about their cases, particularly one child who, they said, would certainly die if she were moved. They were brutally told to obey orders, and some were beaten, and the internees had to remain where they were.

Sonè was obviously in a mad rage, for as the women

passed in front of him, he kicked them with his army boots or hit them over the head. Many fainted from the heat and cruel treatment, but attempts to help them only led to further punishment, and we just had to stand and endure it.

Other Japanese officers who had been called out looked supremely bored by the whole proceedings, though this did not stop them beating up women when they felt like it. At last, at ten o'clock at night, the parade was dismissed. I rushed back to the bungalow, for I was terribly worried about Deborah and Ferne. For once even a Japanese doctor had to admit that she was obviously very ill, and she was allowed to drag herself back with Ferne at midnight. We tried to eat some cold rice, and went to our mattresses, wondering what on earth had caused such a punishment. Later we heard that Tokyo had been bombed on the 26th, and after this we were able to relate most of our bad punishments to Allied bombings or other Japanese losses.

When the women of mixed birth were sent off to Kramat, for a short time we had more room in our bungalow, and I had been able to move Deborah and Ferne from the tiny storeroom they'd previously used at the back of the bungalow to a pleasanter front room. The store had been right up against the stockade, and the guards made a dreadful noise going their rounds, and used the outer wall as a lavatory when they felt like it. Sometimes, though, they could prove a blessing, as on one occasion when Deborah and I were sitting up late talking, and a shower of cigarettes suddenly landed on our laps over the stockade. We were absolutely amazed, and delighted, and though slightly dubious as

–

to whether the cigarettes were safe to smoke or not, we didn't waste much time in finding out!

This fear of being poisoned was often in our minds, and had made many people nervous when we had been forced to have vaccinations in the prison and many of us wondered if we were being used as human guinea pigs. Like other things during internment, perhaps this now sounds far-fetched, but when you have lived for months in a state of fear and tension and under absolute orders from men who sometimes behaved like wild animals, it was very easy to get strange ideas.

Whilst I'm on this subject, I should also mention another thing which upset a lot of women, both in Lengkong and later. The Japanese told us that after a year women who did not live with their husbands were divorced, and that at the end of the first year in Bandoeng we were divorced. Most of us didn't worry about it, but a few who were unhappily married, or knew their husbands had been unfaithful, had an added worry. Some of the older women, too, who should have known better, spread stories about the percentage of men who became impotent in the '14–'18 war. One old woman, who had nursed in Germany in that war, for some reason took real pleasure in torturing the young wives and telling them 'their husbands were without doubt being supplied with women in their camps.'

In fact, I later learned that the vast majority of the men, like the women, were in too low a state of vitality to take an interest in sex, and, like us, only hoped to keep alive from day to day. Nevertheless, some of the women in Tjideng were made doubly unhappy by the stories, even though they knew the woman who spread them was one of the biggest liars in the camp. Still, even she had good points, and notwithstanding her sharp tongue, she helped Lydia Leslie with the twins and her two older children all through internment, and was at least partly responsible for keeping them moderately clean and well-behaved. Lydia herself was artistic, and would often keep children amused making little boats from the skin of the papaya fruit, but she was completely hopeless about organization, so that the twins were constantly being looked after by someone else. She would spend hours trying to boil a pan of water on the side of the huge rice drums to make it absolutely hygienic, whilst the twins trailed round the bungalow with nappies coated in filth from dysentery, and a fly-covered bit of sugary biscuit in their hands.

There were in fact several such women in our group, always kind-hearted and ready to give someone else a helping hand, but unable to look after their own children or finish a string of jobs with which they had become bored.

On the day following the punishment, we were squeezed into fewer bungalows to make room for the hundreds more internees arriving from the Bandoeng camps. Eventually Tjideng contained over eight thousand women and children. Suddenly the Japanese gave orders that all open spaces were to be broken up and planted with vegetables, which must be growing when a high officer visited the camp in six weeks.

In vain the block leaders protested that it was not only impossible to break up the tarmac, but that we had no tools to do the work. The only answer they got was: 'Six weeks General come. Vegetables growing.'

For the next six weeks we worked like maniacs breaking up the dry hard earth from the open compounds in the camp, and the tarmac roads running through such spaces. In the heat of the afternoon, for of course all the ordinary work of the camp had to continue, two women went from each house to break up the dry lumps of clay which had been broken with a sort of mattock in the morning.

I frequently squatted next to Bertie van Mook, both of us using old broken knives to chop up the hard clay, and though she was often ill, nothing daunted her. She was always cheerful and did her full share, and even more than that, of work in the bungalow and outside. I always had a great admiration for her, and had known her before the war when she and her husband stayed in Soebang. As I mentioned earlier, she had elected to stay behind when her husband, the Acting Governor General, was ordered out by the Dutch Government.

Eventually the hard ground was broken up, watered from the sewage ditches beside the roads, and planted with vegetables. In six weeks' time, as ordered, the vegetables were growing when the Japanese General arrived.

13

Hospital Cook

When we were forced to move into a smaller allocation of bungalows, I went to a different one from Deborah, and instead of being house leader went to work in the hospital kitchen. In fact, I had been doing both jobs for a time, with Deborah helping me with making lists and other things, but in the end it got too much. I also found we were having rows over her state of health, and whether she would not be better in hospital. As I didn't want to break our friendship, I decided it was better to move in to another bungalow.

The hospital kitchen was run by a Mrs Mollinger who, with her daughter, had been very kind to Deborah, and I was glad to work for her. The kitchen was to one side of the main building, and consisted of one shed with two tables in it, and a sunken pit, lined roughly with bricks, to which one descended by four steep steps. The two ovens in this pit were stocked with wood, and drums and *wadjangs* stood on iron sheets over the flames. It was hot and heavy work, especially as the rains had not started properly, but when they did arrive we cursed, for the water poured along the ground and down into the fire pits, making it very difficult to do any cooking at all.

Added to this, the Japanese either could not, or would not, work the sluice gates in the canal which surrounded the camp, so that when the heavy rains fell we were flooded to a depth of two or three feet. Apart from the horrible job of wading, our legs covered with sores, through knee-deep streams of sewage to get to work, there was always the danger of missing the edge of the road, and drowning in the deep drains on either side.

One night the rain fell in torrents, and as we lay crowded together in the bungalows, those of us who had been lent beds were joined by those who had none, as the water rose and flooded the whole street. The rains stopped just before the filthy sewage reached bed level, but it took a long time before the houses could be cleaned, and they could not be dried out at all, for the rains continued for the next few months. Apparently the Japanese learned to work the sluices after that, for such a flood never happened again, at any rate whilst I was still at Tjideng.

Work in the hospital kitchen normally began after morning rollcall, but if meat or other special food had come in, we were excused and could go and start the fires earlier.

A dozen of us worked in a squad, and whilst some stoked the rapidly burning wood fires, others prepared the vegetables and meat – if there was any – and then started cooking the various dishes. The rice was cooked separately, and was an art in itself – something in which I was thoroughly instructed by the end of internment.

In a shed next door to us was another squad working in the diet kitchen, and they were responsible for the thin rice porridge and other such dishes which was all that the camp could produce in the way of light diet. They also apportioned the chilli sauce to those patients who needed it, though this might equally have applied to us all, for we were then suffering badly from lack of vitamins and getting many diseases, including tuberculosis, dysentery and mumps, and the death rate was steadily rising.

By December, 1944, it was about eight per day, and as there were at times insufficient coffins, boxes had to be used, into which the bodies had to be broken or squeezed as decently as possible. The Japanese provided a bunch of bananas to go on a coffin, which was a temptation to anyone who saw it, and one of the office staff was allowed to go to the cemetery. It was a horrible task, but necessary, as it afforded our only chance to look at the men's plot and see the names of those who had died recently.

Usually in the case of a woman losing a relation, she was called to the office and the Japanese in charge told her that her husband, brother or son was dead, and handed her a small package containing hair and fingernail cuttings. If it was humanly possible, it was wiser to show no emotion, for the Japanese disliked any display of feeling, and were frequently cruel to any woman who cried.

Another cruel trick was to give a man the choice of having such hair and nail cuttings sent to his wife, or be executed as a punishment for some crime. One Dutchwoman I knew received such a summons, and many months later found it hard to believe her daughter who, in peeping through the *bilik*, saw her father working on a Bandoeng street-cleaning duty. Only after the war was the poor woman able to establish the fact that her husband was indeed alive after all.

We had proof of Japanese anger when emotion was shown a few months earlier in Tjideng, when an order was circulated that all dogs were to be brought to the main gate for removal. I did not go to the gate myself, and felt very sorry for the children who had to lose precious pets. I had had to leave my horse in Soebang, and learned he had been brutally butchered by the looting crowds.

The first women to take their dogs were politely received, and the animals loaded on to freight cars, but as more and more women and children arrived and showed emotion, the Japanese got furious, and finally beat and kicked the dogs on to the truck, many in a dying condition. A dreadful scene followed, and some of the internees received severe punishment, which could have been avoided if only the block leaders had taken the dogs to the gate.

Conditions towards the end of December were awful, and cooking became daily more difficult. It was seldom we received meat, but occasionally the Japanese sent in offal which was sometimes so high by the time it reached us that it had to be refused, though this was only done when it was absolutely impossible for human consumption, and by this time our standards were not high.

On Christmas Day I received a message that I was needed to help clean offal in the hospital kitchen. As usual the Japanese sent the stuff in late in the afternoon – they ignored Sundays or holidays – and as we had nightly blackouts by then, when all the fires had to be out, there was not much time for cleaning and cooking the offal.

As soon as I got to the shed – no one else had arrived – I started a fire and put on one of the huge drums of water to boil, and began to clean the offensive mess.

Every cat in the neighbourhood arrived, but still no humans, and I cleaned the most disgusting collection of entrails, testicles and organs I have ever seen. Eventually the lights-out signal went, and I had to finish alone in the dark. As I hurriedly cut up the revolting eleven kilos of filth, I was furiously angry, and felt very sorry for myself being left with such a horrible job on Christmas night. Eventually, however, my sense of humour got the better of me, and I remembered a book of Harry Graham's poems which had amused me long before, about a girl who quarrelled with her boyfriend whilst dining at the Ritz. I couldn't remember much of the poem, but the lines, 'The tears she was too proud to wipe went trickling down into the tripe,' stuck in my memory, and I had to laugh, angry as I was.

In January Mrs Mollinger and her daughter were moved to another camp, and the kitchen was run by another woman from Singapore, who was already in Tjideng when we arrived. Mrs Murray was nearly as good a cook as Mrs Mollinger, but she unfortunately had not the same control over the cooking squad, and far too much food disappeared. This gave the kitchen a bad name, and the hospital patients complained that the food they should have had was going to make the kitchen staff fat.

There was some truth in this, and some of the squad were far from skinny, though this was possibly due to quite another cause. Whilst many of us at this time had swollen faces, legs and bodies from oedema, many others were suffering from lack of menstruation, and appeared abnormally puffy and swollen. The greater number of women I knew failed to menstruate after the first months in camp, which in a way was a blessing as

we had no pads or cloths to use. After the war I heard
that this is a normal occurrence when women are under
stress.

I continued with the squad until January, when I had
a bad go of fever and had to give up. In many ways I
was not sorry, as the feeling in the squad altered after
Mrs Mollinger left, and I did not like working with
people I could not trust.

In Tjideng someone gave me a notebook and pencil,
and under 9 January I wrote: 'The most extraordinary
thing happened yesterday. I had fever for three days,
and although I had more or less recovered, I kept seeing
pictures of every shape all day.'

This in itself was not unusual, but everything turned
into shapes. I'd been given a massage by one of the
women to stop my headache, but couldn't sleep
because of the noise. After lights out I started to see
pictures on the wall, not made up by me – at least, not
consciously – but flickering over in thousands, and all
more or less connected with water. Sometimes sea, or
a shining river, or other small streams full of queer
baskets of green plants, or mechanical devices. I could
see the pictures equally well with my eyes open or
shut, but if I tried to see something special, then
everything faded at once.

After a while I felt my husband holding my hand,
and we watched the pictures together. I badly wanted
to see the children – where they were and how they
looked after all these years – but for a long time this
only shut them off. I saw thousands of these snaps,
some of which I could not understand, and lots of
which were made up of ugly, grimacing faces. Many

others were of beautifully clothed figures and magnificently staged.

A huge army of men, with the lower part of their faces covered, I recognized as our own men from the Company, and saw Gordon, Corney and some others I've forgotten. No picture returned again, however much I tried to remember it. I was worried the men's faces were covered, until I realized they were shouting and cheering, only hadn't shaved and didn't want me to see! Much later on, still amongst terrible ruins and curious scenes laid out as if I flew over them, shapes appeared cut in paper and stitched like countries, or as sets of dolls to represent different things – cooking round a fire and so on. Everything went so fast it was difficult to remember. Then I saw a rush of girls running down a hill with trees on it, and knew Daphne was there, and after some time I saw her in a bright green dress playing a piano in a big hall, with two plaits down her back. She only turned from her music for a moment, and smiled.

Jane was much more difficult to see, but Mr and Mrs Miller rushed up twice, cheering hard each time, and then I saw Jane, looking long legged and, I think, with a fringe.

I could not see Charles, perhaps naturally, and at the end of nearly all the changing pictures I saw a photo of King George VI and heard the National Anthem, whereupon I wept. I tried hard to find some special date, but nothing came. When all was finished, I understood – by a voice, I think – that I was better and must rest and then go out and help others.

It will be seen from the above how our minds were not only on our families but when the war would end.

In all the camps we had fortune tellers, though the sad thing was that those women who had a genuine gift were pressed so hard by anxious women that in the end they made up what they thought was wanted. This was not so with Farida in Tanah Tinggi prison, since she only came into the prison for having told the Japanese what she believed to be true, and what later turned out to be correct.

There were also women of no gift, who were unscrupulous in telling fortunes to get hold of extra portions of food – the usual fee.

All that Farida told me, to my surprise came true after the war; and a man I met later in Batavia had the same ability. He also, in prison, was able by looking at a picture to tell what was happening to that person, though some of the things he saw were not pleasant.

14
Culinary Art

Although I had been obliged to give up cooking in the hospital kitchen, as soon as I got over the fever I was able to take turns weekly with the woman who was cooking in the bungalow where I lived, as she had also been ill, and was feeling the strain of camp life very much. She and her family of five children lived in an old garage, and during wet weather, like many others in the camp, she had a terrible cough.

Many internees had gone down with tuberculosis in various forms, and there were few who did not suffer from beri-beri caused by the perpetual rice diet, oedema brought about by general malnutrition, dysentery or pellagra. This last sickness had attacked many women. It took the form of angry reddish-brown marks like burns over the skin, very often in the form of a butterfly, from which, I think, it got its Italian name. This skin burn, which was also caused by the lack of the right food, very often came first on the face, particularly the nose, as well as attacking hands and feet, and it was of the greatest importance that the sufferer should not expose herself to the sun, which aggravated the burns and could ultimately lead to insanity.

When it suited them, the Japanese disregarded any form of sickness, so they had no scruples in ordering everyone to work in the 'gardens', whether fit or not, and as the internees also had to stand for hours of the day in queues or rollcall, this particular sickness made great strides.

Except for dysentery, which everyone had in one form or another, and some fever, I had kept pretty fit – perhaps because I sweated so hard. This wasn't always a blessing, for though it may have kept me healthy, it certainly rotted what few clothes I had far more quickly. Had it not been for the women from our Company, and other friends, who very quickly supplied me, and many others, with things when I went to Tjideng, I should have been literally in rags.

I was given a strong pair of shorts, two shirts, and three dresses, which made an extensive wardrobe, and one dress – a white silk one – which I kept for special occasions. We had all tried to keep one dress 'for when we get free', but very few of the British had been able to save anything, and of course we were mostly shoeless.

Few of us had any soap, disinfectant or face cream, though apparently the British were in the minority about this. I was continually amazed both in Tjideng and later in Kampong Makassar to find that some internees, particularly the French, had wonderful cosmetics until the very end of the war. Perhaps they preferred to fill their suitcases with them, rather than food, as being better for morale, and maybe they had a point.

Nevertheless, the question of food began to figure very largely in most people's thoughts, as more and more women used what bits of paper they had to write out recipes, and plan fine dinners which apparently helped to appease their ever-growing hunger.

I had never collected recipes – probably because I

wanted what paper I could lay my hands on for
cigarettes or writing – but in Tjideng I was given a large
notebook by a Dutch girl, and was then able to collect
recipes of dishes from women of all nationalities. I
never lost it – until after the war – so had a fine book
of individually tested recipes from women in all parts
of the world.

Except for teaching my young Soendanese cook in
Soebang – and he took to it like a duck to water – I
really cared little about it, but with the help of a woman
from the Soerabaja British, who had lived in Java all
her life, I enjoyed doing the house cooking on alternate
weeks. At the time there were forty-five of us in our
bungalow.

Two of the young girls cooked the rice, and I did the
trimmings, and as we still occasionally got fish, we
were able to make broth and all sorts of dishes.

Everything was flavoured with the native spices,
which helped to make the otherwise insipid food
appetizing.

The Swiss woman who had been in my room at
Tangarang was in the same bungalow, and as she loved
to interfere in everything, and was greedy, she continually hung round the charcoal fire. I was determined
she should not learn my culinary secrets, and refused
quite childishly to let her help me. We were all getting
on one another's nerves, and the fact that for two and a
quarter years we had been without peace or privacy –
except for the short time we were locked in cells – was
beginning to tell.

The woman from the Soerabaja group was a great
help, and went over the vegetables and spices which
were brought from the market weekly, suggesting vari-

ous menus, and explaining carefully how such dishes should be made.

The spices had to be used with the greatest care, for they had to last four weeks. Unless the cook did use them sparingly, and some did not, the cook for the third or last period would have nothing with which to flavour her rice, sweet potatoes or cabbage, which would bring down the curses of the house on her head. Charcoal also had to be rationed with care, and this all depended on the leader of the house, who could save many rows by keeping an eye on everything and taking a firm line from the start. Luckily the bungalow I went to had a good head, though she was unpopular with many of the British because of her sharp tongue, and for being over-friendly with the Japanese.

I worked with her on many occasions – she was Dutch by birth – and though she certainly did manage to get a lot out of the Japanese, I think this was due to the way she tackled them and not to any over-friendliness on her part. She was an extremely shrewd woman, but I never found anything objectionable about her, and when taken at her own value she could be most amusing.

She was never afraid of hard work, and even if she did put her own family first when it came to allotting things, I suppose this was only human under the circumstances. She at least had the courage of her convictions and was never afraid to speak up to the Japanese when she thought we had been badly treated.

15

The Night Watch

Two things made Tjideng different from our three previous camps. Some of the Dutch had a great many books to lend us – one woman was reputed to have taken seventeen *sado*-loads of books and luggage into one of the Bandoeng camps! – and secondly, if we were trusted by those with radios we were able to get news. Though the camp was searched many times, and very heavy punishment given if a radio was found, a few remained hidden.

After some months the first mail was allowed in, although it was dated 1942. I heard for certain that Jane and the other families had arrived safely in Perth, Western Australia, and that at that time Daphne was well in England. Neither Charles nor I ever had a letter from Jane, but in Tanah Tinggi I'd received a card (twenty-five words in Malay) from him, and sent one postcard to him and one to Daphne.

Since we were permitted to send only one postcard in six months, and that concession only came after the first year and if the Japanese were in a conciliatory mood, it was hard to decide whom to write to. Having tried one (in Malay) to Charles, and one of three obligatory sentences in English to Daphne, I sent the third to Jane. I just hoped Charles wouldn't worry at not hearing from me, but in the event needn't have distressed myself. With the exception of the note I had

–

taken to Soeka Miskin myself, he got no word from me
until three months before release.

The Japanese played a particularly dirty trick on the
men, by allowing them to write their postcards, only to
have the cards discovered stacked in a cupboard six
months later when Bill Leslie, Lydia's husband, was
working in the prison office. His captors were much
amused.

Both conditions and the temper of the Japanese in
Tjideng had deteriorated by the end of 1944. We had a
blackout each night, and since there was little material
with which to cover our lights, it was a source of added
fear to the British group.

One night when we'd done the best we could with
cardboard and an old *sarong* I'd been given, we heard
the guard coming along the street, followed by the
well-known sloff-sloff of Japanese boots. The feet
stopped outside our door. When the guard came in and
said we were showing too much light, I hastily
explained we'd done the best we could, but the candel-
abra shape made it difficult. In stormed a Japanese, and
most of the forty occupants of the bungalow huddled
in a corner in fear of what might happen.

We were not left long in doubt. He ordered me to get
on the chair and arrange the *sarong*, or at least by his
shouts and gestures I guessed that was what he wanted,
and I did as he told me. Apparently it was not satisfactory, and I got down, and to my absolute horror he then
got up on the rickety chair. It was a worm-eaten one
I had been glad enough to have as we had nothing to
sit on.

The stocky Japanese climbed up. I watched terrified.

It stood the strain, but the Japanese was no better at arranging the blackout than I had been, so he shouted with rage and pulled the whole light out of the ceiling and threw it at me, hitting me in the face. In future we were to have no light.

The blackout caused a nuisance in another way, as thieving of clothes, food and even vegetables we had planted was a growing worry. Shortages of food were by then serious, so as well as many more vegetables planted in the camp, we'd put in papayas and other fruit trees alongside the roads. With many hundreds more women and children crammed into the camp, search was impossible, and we were ordered to start night patrols, one woman from every bungalow, working in pairs, by shifts.

As far as the clothing thefts were concerned, we thought it was also done by guards and others who came over the stockades at night. In the blackout it was impossible to tell, and as the natives came over in loin cloths, and often greased, we couldn't have caught them. We had to try somehow, but the thought of tackling a practically nude, greased native probably armed with a knife, had little appeal. When I could I paired with Greet, a young Dutch girl who, with her mother, we'd known in Tanah Tinggi. She was near Daphne's age, so I enjoyed talking to her.

Some nights we were on duty in the empty market, and on others had to patrol up and down the streets in the dark – frequently in heavy rain, too – and along the stockade which bounded the railway track.

The third place we patrolled was the vegetable garden, and when it rained and we had only wooden *klompen* to wear, they stuck in the thick mud or the strap over the toes broke. It became increasingly difficult to repair a break, since we'd neither nails, cloth nor bits of rubber to make a new strap. I dreaded having to walk in bare feet in the sticky mud, not only because of snakes, but also because the garden was the most likely place to pick up ringworm.

We were not allowed a torch, though there was light in the main market, where we reported. If it poured with rain we could shelter, provided the Japanese didn't catch us, as they doled out punishment if one was caught off duty.

I most hated coming off shift, since I still feared the dark, and often had to return to the market or back to the bungalow through the sleeping camp alone if Greet and I were on different shifts. Sometimes we were switched on the midnight and four o'clock duties.

The Japanese also patrolled the camp at night, of course, either on bikes without lights or in rubber soled shoes. There would be a sudden yell in the dark, and a torch flashed on one's face before one was allowed to continue. It was singularly unpleasant, especially as all Japanese carried revolvers, and used them more quickly as tempers worsened.

Only one thing pleased me, and that was the beauty and peace of the camp on a fine night. Because of overcrowding, the crying of little children and the shrill, disturbed voices of women never ceased, so that it was impossible to make up lost sleep during the day.

Since Deborah slept only fitfully, usually I tried to have a few words with her before turning in. Ferne, luckily, continued to thrive despite the appalling conditions in which she was being brought up. She kept us endlessly amused with her tricks, but didn't talk much. Hardly surprising, I suppose, since the poor kid heard so many languages during the day. She made up for it by being a complete little individual, and letting us know in no uncertain manner what she wanted.

When the three of us were together, we tried to forget for a little while the horror in which we lived.

—

16

The Last Move

It was the end of January, 1945, when rumours began to fly round that we were to be moved, and I was worried I might be moved and Deborah left – as well as by the fact that I had jaundice.

At first we did not realize this unpleasant complaint was infectious, but later women were isolated where possible, and given sugar – if there was any to spare. I went to the woman doctor at the end of our road, who by this time was without medicines, but she gave me a tiny tin of sugar – I'm sure from her own small stock, bless her – which later helped me a lot.

I had stayed on my mattress for two days, feeling pretty ill, when orders came from the Japanese that we were to parade in the main street. After standing for some time, Sonè and some officers, including doctors, came out and sat under the trees. Several of the British group were called out, and told to stand apart, and also many from the Dutch groups, until about five hundred of us had been chosen. Not all of these had been called specifically, but where a daughter was named, the mother and sisters often volunteered to join her, so that they should not be parted.

We were told to report the following morning, and though I was copper yellow with jaundice and many of the women chosen were far sicker than I was, we apparently had one thing in common, and that was that though our legs were in many cases covered with ulcers, they had not yet swollen from oedema, or at any rate not sufficiently to be noticed by the Japanese.

Several Dutchwomen did not want to be moved, for by this time we had gathered that we were being sent to a work camp, and bandaged their legs or otherwise faked illness. Sonè was not caught by anything so simple as that, and had the bandages off in a moment, cursing the offenders.

For some reason I had been made to stand alone, but was later joined by about five Dutchwomen. We never did discover why we were segregated, but I did not like it, for it meant that I might be sent to a different place, or at any rate not with my own group. As we had stuck together for so long, I had hoped we should be able to do so till the end of the war.

After standing for some time with the hot sun blazing down on us, I felt faint, and asked the Japanese if I might sit down, to which they agreed and I got a little wooden stool under a tree. When I was called up to be examined by the doctor, he merely glanced at my legs, taking no notice of my jaundiced face, and told me I passed.

Tjideng was so dreadful by this time that had it not been for Deborah, Ferne and other friends, I should have been glad to go. Anyhow, it was impossible to argue, and those of us who were chosen for the work camp, and those who had volunteered, were told to be ready to move. We did not, of course, know where we were to be taken, but supposed it might be somewhere near Batavia, as so many women's camps had been brought there from other parts of Java, and our job apparently was to grow vegetables for those camps.

At any rate, we very much hoped we might be

somewhere near the sea, so that we might at least have some fresh air, for the smell of Tjideng with its open drains, sickness and rotting vegetation, and the uncleared sewage, was appalling.

For the rest of the day I tried to take things fairly easily, but had to try to see as many friends as possible, and I felt miserable leaving so many sick behind. Of our original Bandoeng group, at least twenty were on the very sick list, and a further six dead or dying. As this was only one small part of the original Lengkong group, and that an infinitesimal part of the whole camp, where the deaths were proportionately high, the general feeling of great depression, and even despair, will be readily understood.

By far my greatest worry was the thought of Deborah, Ferne and I being parted. Ever since we had met in Tanah Tinggi prison, Deborah and I had remained firm friends, and looked after little Ferne together. In Tjideng there were many other people ready to help them, but the thought that I was being taken to another camp and might never see Deborah and Ferne again was deeply upsetting.

At midnight the five hundred of us who were leaving said goodbye for the last time to our friends, some of whom we were never to see again, and with sad hearts climbed into the waiting lorries. There was the usual shouting by the Japanese, and frenzied last-minute checking by the office, but as I crawled on to the end of a full lorry, with my bucket and hat-box which contained all my possessions except my mattress and blanket, I was too ill to care where we went, and only managed to stick where I was because a Dutch girl held my arm. The lorry flap was then shut, and a Japanese soldier sat on my bucket, amusing himself from time to time by pinching my bottom. Even this I was too sick to resent, which was perhaps just as well, for there were twenty-five of us standing in the lorry, which left little room for manoeuvre. Also the Japanese were always specially nervous when they moved us from camp to camp, even though this was usually done at dead of night, and sick though I was, I had no wish to be spitted with a bayonet.

We shivered as we drove out through Batavia in the cold night air, though fortunately it had stopped raining, and arrived at our new camp, which lay on the main road out to Buitenzorg, at about two o'clock in the morning.

After we had turned off the main road, and passed through large gates with sentries beside them, and driven about five more minutes along a bumpy, greasy cart track, the long convoy of lorries jolted to a standstill. Thick clouds scudded across the sky, and the moonlight caught and glistened on hundreds of coconut palms, but that was all there was time to see before we were ordered to get down and stand in groups.

One by one each group was led past a large, old-fashioned bungalow, which blazed with unshaded lights, and on through a barbed wire fence. Once past the bungalow, it was dark again, and all we could see were rows and rows of long bamboo huts, built round the trunks of palm trees. At intervals the palm trees stuck out of the roofs, which were made of palm leaves.

As it was the middle of the wet season, the ground was a sea of sticky mud, and we slithered and slipped along the narrow paths by deep trenches that had been dug alongside each hut. The whole camp appeared to

—

be a network of such trenches, which were crossable at intervals and in doorways by small, slippery bamboo bridges.

In the semi-darkness, for the moon kept disappearing, we wondered where we were being taken, and as each great length of hut had only one or two small unshaded electric lights, the whole effect was gloomy in the extreme. Nevertheless, it did not stop us from seeing that as usual the bamboo *bali-balis* which formed the sleeping-platforms were simply alive with bugs.

I was in a Dutch group, and as most of them had never been in any other camp than Tjideng, they thought we were being led to our houses by way of the cow stalls. They soon learned their mistake, for the Japanese led us to the fourth hut in the row and left us. As the conditions were little different from Tangarang, except that the floor of the hut was mud, and the walls plaited bamboo, and as by then I was feeling pretty ill, I humped my small amount of luggage on the platform and lay down. Some time later we got our mattresses, and I put mine in my allotted span – at this time about one and a half metres per person – spread my ancient sheet and blanket, and tried to sleep.

The following morning I found not one square inch of the sheet without bug marks, and we were all covered in bites and blood. Many of the internees had never lived in such circumstances, and were simply horrified. There was nothing to do but begin the rather hopeless task of trying to clean up the huts.

For the first days I had to stick to the barracks, but those British who had been sent to the camp came to see me, and Corrie, the tall, thin Dutch girl who had helped me on the lorry, was very kind and gave me a hand.

The morning after we arrived in Kampong Makassar, ill or not, we were all summoned to a large open playing field, in the second half of the camp, and addressed by a Japanese official. We were told that we had been brought to the camp (the name, like that of many other prison camps in Java, was intended to mislead outsiders who might hear about us into believing we had been moved to Macassar, on Celebes, one of the other islands of Indonesia) to work in the vegetable gardens. Only a part of the camp was being used, and we would be paid for the work, the highest pay being fifteen cents per day, and this money would be used by us to buy goods from a camp shop.

The Japanese said that the running of the camp would be left to us, but of course under their control, and he asked for volunteers to work in the office. Hereupon the Swiss woman whom I disliked stepped forward and said she would be head of the camp. A Dutchwoman, who was charming but later proved to be too kind-hearted, joined her, and after arranging for others to work in the office, a staff was formed.

I had to go back to my hut after this, and didn't take much interest in anything for a few days, and meantime the camp got organized.

The second night was made hideous by the arrival in our barracks of a large, semi-tame monkey, which belonged either to the troops who had recently left Kampong Makassar, or to the Japanese. The two dim lights in the hut showed very little, and suddenly at about eleven o'clock there was a blood-curdling yell from near the main doorway. We all sat up – and a ghastly sight most of the dishevelled, unhappy women looked as they lay side by side in two long rows – and saw to our horror a large grey monkey jumping from place to place, and pulling at covers and buckets as he jumped.

The more the women struck at him in their fear, the more angry he became, and only those who had managed to stretch some sort of mosquito net over themselves felt at all protected. One woman opened a paper sunshade to shoo the beast away, and he simply gibbered with rage. Finally, rather nervously, the head of the hut was sent to fetch the police guard, who came grudgingly, and kicked the beast away with their large boots, so that he did not come near us again.

Throughout the night there were squeaks and shrieks as the rats ran up and down the bamboos, trying to find any food which might have been left uncovered.

Nevertheless, with all its disadvantages, Kampong Makassar did not seem to me too bad after Tjideng, despite the muddy huts in which we were to live. At least there was plenty of fresh air – too much at times – and we were all more than thankful to be away from Sonè, and for a time from any children, though the majority of us were extremely worried over the fate of family or friends we had left behind.

17
Kampong Makassar

The camp consisted of fourteen huts, each meant to contain up to three hundred men, though when we were moved in we only used four huts at first, and half the camp, including the large parade ground, was completely wired off. Nevertheless, some of the barracks had fairly large spaces between them, and although we were surrounded by the usual high stockade and police boxes, on stilts, we did have a much larger open space and greater feeling of freedom than ever before.

The long bamboo barracks, built along the rows of palm trees, had roofs made out of the palm leaves, so when it rained during the next four months, the water poured in, and ran along the rafters and down the trunks of the palms. It also teemed in torrents down the sloping mud floor of the huts, and woe betide anyone who unwisely left *klompen* on the ground on a rainy night – they would have floated off by morning. Our *klompen* were invaluable, when they did not break at a critical moment, for by then they were the only footwear many of us had, and kept us off the filthy floor of the lavatories, apart from their use for ordinary work around the camp. Consequently to lose a pair – and they quickly disappeared if allowed out of one's sight for a moment – was a serious matter.

Down the centre of each hut was a narrow gangway, and as most of the Dutchwomen had two or three cabin trunks of food and clothes with them, the limited space was rapidly used up. There was a good deal of squabbling about the amount of room per person, and whether the bamboo platforms were strong enough to take heavy trunks, but eventually things were sorted out. Most of the people in the barracks I was in had material, and proceeded to put up a cloth or sheet to divide them from their next-door neighbour, in order to have some privacy.

After some days, the barracks had the appearance of a gypsy encampment, but for those who slept towards the centre of the hut, the lack of air was a great disadvantage, and extra holes were cut in the plaited bamboo walls, though when the Japanese saw this ventilation spoiling their beautiful huts they got very annoyed.

Between every three or four huts was a washroom of *balik*, open at one end and containing a water barrel and a few taps. The upper part of the walls was left open under a bamboo leaf, so that the wind whistled in. At first many of the Dutch found it hard to take community showers, but soon got used to it just as we had done at Tanah Tinggi. In the end the washroom was a pleasant place where one heard all the latest gossip and rumours, and a great deal more as well. We also found it conducive to singing, but the Japanese objected and threatened to come in and beat us up if we did not stop, which was a pity.

The big kitchen and store sheds were up near the camp entrance, and were much like Lengkong, though larger. When we went to Makassar we were given five drums for the five hundred of us, which had to be used both for rice and vegetable cooking, and it was found we could only manage by cooking the rice during the night and the vegetables in the day.

Cooking arrangements were difficult enough anyway, for at Makassar a wall about three feet high had been built in the kitchen, with six spaces left for wood fires, so one had to climb up over broken brick and cement to lift the heavy drums up on to the fires. Many people were badly burned during the next months, and many more hurt through slipping into the greasy, deep air-raid trenches. Since the majority of women were brought in to work in the vegetable garden, not many could be spared for cooking, but squads were formed under suitable cooks and the life of the camp began.

As well as the kitchen, there was a bakery shed, with two large ovens, but at first it was not used and very nasty rubbery bread was sent in from outside.

Several women doctors and dentists had come with the five hundred, and after the first month when many women lost a great deal of weight, we were ordered to be weighed monthly. Originally, we had only a small clinic and consulting room, but later one of the huts had to be turned into a hospital to cope with the large number of seriously sick.

The sanitary arrangements were also much the same as at Lengkong, except that as there was no covered way to the sheds, those with dysentery had to creep out of the hut at night in pouring rain, cross a large open quagmire of red mud, carrying a tin or half a coconut full of water to cleanse themselves, and then wait in turn to squat over one of the holes.

Because our only lighting came from the large arc lights in the sentry boxes, and a dim lamp at the end of each hut, it was difficult to see the way, and as one's

klompen usually broke or stuck in the mud, the journey
to and from the pest hole was horrible. After several
such trips each night, coming back wetter in the down-
pour each time, one crept despairingly up on to the
bamboo platform, and probably spent the rest of the
night killing bugs.

Every morning the whole camp attended rollcall on
the road near the entrance gate, and those who worked
in the gardens were counted off, and let out through
the barbed wire. The first morning I was well enough
to go to *appel*, I heard that the wretched monkey which
had frightened us the first night was roving about, and
that some of the women had already been bitten by
him. When we were all lined up and the Japanese and
the head of the camp had already started down the
rows – we had already bowed and were standing to
attention – I heard muffled sounds near me, and saw
women flapping wildly at the monkey. He came along
the line, and stopped by me, putting his paw out to
touch my leg, and as I was in very short shorts, a ragged
shirt and *klompen* I felt rather a nude target. The
monkey chattered a bit, and then took a grip on my
bare leg, and started to climb up me. I was absolutely
paralysed, partly because I had once had the terrible
injections against rabies when my cat died of it and I
feared a second dose, but I at least stayed still through
fright, and, when he was holding on round my waist,
managed to tell him to go down. Probably as I was so
frightened I didn't speak loudly, for he was an
extremely hefty animal standing about two feet high,
but he fortunately decided to do what he was told.

Shortly afterwards he sprang upon a young girl, and
she, poor little thing, screamed, and was badly bitten

on the cheek. Then there was a great commotion, and at last the Japanese went after the monkey and shot it. We were very thankful, for most of us had lived long enough out East to know what happened when bitten if we could not get injections.

I was still not well enough to work in the gardens, and because of pellagra, and the danger involved, was forbidden by the doctor to go out in the sun if I could avoid it, so volunteered for work in the barracks fetching meals from the cook-house, washing clothes for people who were ill and other jobs. One of these was converting dresses into shorts, which made the most practical wear for camp, so I sat like a tailor on the platform in my spare time doing a nice line in internees' smart camp wear.

The work in the barracks was supposed to be light, but in fact fetching the food was extremely heavy and sometimes dangerous. Between times one could rest, and as the majority of the women were away most of the morning and afternoon in the gardens, the huts were beautifully peaceful. A library had also been started with the pooled books brought in by the Dutch, and those of us interested revelled in it.

I worked in the hut with Corrie. Both she and her mother were ill, the latter to become desperately so later, but Hennie, the younger sister, was able to join the squad of women who looked after the pigs. At first they had to work in bare feet, but subsequently were provided with boots, which was just as well for later they had to kill the pigs themselves with what came to hand. The pigs were small but fierce, and the killing was horrendous.

Corrie, being tall, rapidly became 'Tiny', and though

she was still weak she never shirked work, though at times the strain must have been great.

At 7 A.M. we went to the kitchen shed and, with the help of two others, fetched a zinc bath of boiled water or weak tea, and the rubbery bread, which had to be dealt out to the hundred occupants of the hut.

In fine weather we could serve the food outside, but when it poured, which it did all the first months until April, we had to give out the food in the barracks. There was very little room for one queue to come to us whilst the served ones walked back to their places. It was also nervous work, since the internees watched like lynxes to see that everyone got the same share – dividing the bread was the worst headache of all. Later we got small loaves of dark maize flour, and were allowed three or four thin slices per person, which had to do for supper and breakfast. The slices were about three by two inches.

After 'breakfast' which, at first, was eked out quite royally by those who had tinned food, we washed out the buckets, and put them away, and then took our laundry to the wash house. I still had two aged sheets, and much to the amusement of the hut, continued to make up my small mattress with them each night. By then the two pairs of pyjamas I had taken into Lengkong were worn out, and also my housecoat, but fortunately someone in Tjideng gave me a kimono and that did duty for both. In fact, it lasted me until the end of the war, though it certainly was in threads by then.

Corrie and I washed for her mother, sister and some girls who worked with the pigs, and ourselves, and then we collected the washing from those who were ill in barracks. She and her family were wonderfully kind to me, insisting on sharing what food they had, as well as invaluable needles, cottons, and most wonderful gift of all, soap.

Unfortunately some of the women we washed for did not give soap, though they often had plenty, and as we were embarrassed to ask in case they had none, Corrie continually used her own supply. When the end of the war came we were shocked and disgusted to see what a store of soap, cigarettes and other goods these women had. Worst of all, those who borrowed money told us quite brazenly afterwards that they had hundreds, sometimes thousands, of guilders hidden in their luggage. Their selfishness, especially to someone like Corrie, revolted me.

Very shortly we also took on the hospital laundry, as they could not get it done, and one day I had a curious experience, when washing the usual collection of towels, nightgowns and sheets. I had just taken a sheet out of my bucket and was washing it, when I saw quite clearly the outline of a woman's head and shoulders on the sheet. I could see that she was dead. Both Corrie and I thought it a little strange, and when I returned the clean washing I asked whether one sheet had been used to cover a body. The nurse looked amazed, then admitted a woman had died the previous day and her sheet had been included in the laundry. When possible the number of deaths was kept secret, as so many internees got further depressed when they heard of the rapid rise in numbers.

By the time we finished the washing, we were soaked in sweat, and had a shower, and then went with the head of the hut to the kitchen to bring back the midday meal. The hut head always collected the special diet of softly boiled rice, and then Corrie and I with two helpers formed a chain carrying the two baskets of cooked rice, a zinc bath of thin vegetable soup and a tin of spiced nuts or vegetables between us. Because the food was very carefully measured out before we left the kitchen we were terrified we should slip in the mud or down one of the trenches before we reached the fourth hut, spilling the soup or boiling water. It was not the thought of the burn which worried us, either, though many carriers were badly scalded, but the thought of how angry the ravenous women would be if they had to go short on the main meal of the day. Fetching the food really did involve great strain, and the buckets and rice baskets – at any rate at first – were very heavy, so that we were thankful when the meal was served, and we could wash out the buckets and pails and settle down to our own meal.

At 2 P.M. the garden workers were ordered out again, unless it was absolutely pouring, when they had the afternoon off – without pay. This was a real blow as it meant they could buy little when the camp store opened.

When the rain was not too heavy to prevent work, the gardeners all swarmed back with the girls from the piggeries at five, covered from head to foot with mud, and shivering with cold. Then they made a rush for the bath-house which was filled with chattering, hungry women, and all they had to appease their hunger until the next morning was two tiny slices of bread and a mug of tea or coffee-water.

Those working with the pigs were sometimes lucky, and ate the pig swill when they could steal it, as well as being able to steal unripe papayas from the fruit trees, though they were searched and punished if caught.

Dusk falls fast in the East, and after talking a while, or joining in a singsong, or maybe a French lesson, we were mostly glad to lie down before lights-out, for it was too dim to sew or read in the barracks. Those who had sleeping-places under a light could gossip or play cards, but the hard work in the camp, and exhaustion from dysentery and other complaints made most internees ready to try at least to get some sleep.

18

Camp Couture

Although we could not be forced to go to work for the Japanese, they only gave extra rations, or pay to buy them with, to those who did so. As the food ration was cut month by month everyone who could stand up did work, for quite apart from hunger it was the best way to keep alive. Those internees who were too weak to do anything, and lay day after day on the bamboo platforms, died. Though the work in the gardens and elsewhere was hard, and the hours much longer than any coolie ever laboured in the fields in Java normally, it nevertheless gave some interest in life, and the companionship was a great help.

The main work in the large vegetable gardens consisted of breaking up the land with *patjols*, the native mattocks, such as we had done in Tjideng, and then cultivating, planting and, in the dry season, endlessly watering the plants. *Kankong*, a coarse-leafed vegetable which grows often by the side of streams in Java, and American spinach, were the two chief vegetables, palatable enough no doubt when eaten in a young state, but ours were old and we had lived on them for two years. Moreover, the *kankong* had very few leaves by the time it reached the kitchen, and we hated the sight of yards of tough, pipe-like leafless stem, though everyone carefully drank the vegetable water, just as we did in Tanah Tinggi, hoping it would do us good.

Tomatoes, red and green chillis, carrots and some

sorts of bean were also grown, together with ground-nuts, though as we grew vegetables for many other prisons and camps besides our own, the greater part of the crop was sent away.

Papaya and other native fruit trees, including bananas, were also planted in the gardens, but whenever a chance occurred the fruit was stolen, though some did get to the hospital.

In May, 1945, the final transference of the Dutch-women's camps from Bandoeng and elsewhere began, and although Kampong Makassar was originally intended as a work camp for women without children, about one thousand five hundred people arrived, over half of them very young children. It is true when we left Tjideng in January one or two internees ordered to the work camp had brought their children with them, but these were all over seven, which was fortunate. The camp with its deep drains and narrow bridges to the huts was a death trap for small children, and a nightmare for all the mothers.

When the first Bandoeng group came staggering in, we were amazed to see dozens of children, and were afterwards told we had looked most hostile, which was probably true.

More huts had been allocated, but we had also been moved up closer in the barracks, and were once again back to a metre per person, which only those from British camps had been used to. I suppose it was natural we looked angry when we saw the women arriving who had caused the trouble, though they, poor things, would obviously much rather have stayed in a cool climate, instead of being sent on a dreadful journey and made to lose their possessions so late in the war.

Some, of course, like ourselves, had left their homes when the Japanese landed, but many were residents of Bandoeng whose houses formed part of a camp, and it was certainly harder to lose one's treasured possessions bit by bit, than to leave them all at once as we had done.

We understood later that in Burma the men had been put in camps by the sea, and the women in the hills, and that when fighting was renewed the men got free and joined the Allies, and the Japanese were determined that this should not happen a second time.

Sometimes I was thankful that I had so little when I saw both Batavia and Bandoeng women staggering along, trying to keep hold of heavy cases containing linen, books, photos, tinned food, and very often clothes for their husbands as well. When the new internees arrived in Kampong Makassar the heavy luggage and mattresses were dumped by the Japanese on the parade ground, and by an unlucky chance that night it simply poured with rain.

The following morning the stricken owners found to their dismay that the torrential rain had ruined a great deal of their stuff. One of the worst losses was ruined photographs, and I felt very much for the newcomers, remembering how angry I had been when my few remaining photos had been stolen in my little blue case.

Although the new barracks had been taken over for our increased numbers, some of the huts had been blown down by the wind and rain, and a squad was formed, mainly of part-Indonesian women, who did a wonderful job building new huts, making and laying a road through camp, and a thousand other repairs. I don't know how we would have managed without them to show us the way.

There was also a tool and repair shed, so that once again it was possible to get a nail or two to mend *klompen* or to stick in a bamboo post, so that one could hang up a wall bag with pockets – the only form of wardrobe we had. I still used Charles's tweed jacket for this, and the pockets were invaluable.

As our clothes after a few months were again getting ragged and torn with the hard work, sweat and constant wear in the sticky red mud which impregnated everything, a sewing party was started in a shed. Clothes could be made or altered by women who understood the work, but were not strong enough to work in the garden or kitchens.

Some of the sights one saw when women set off for the garden or cleaning work were quite staggering. The usual camp dress was a cotton brassière, scanty shorts, clipped hair – and a cigar! We had received no native tobacco for some time, and made a protest in May, after which the Japanese sent in small cheroots. If we wanted to smoke, it had to be cheroots – and this resulted in seeing these strange creatures wandering about the camp. Even more amazing, many of them wore the most beautiful jewellery – one woman I remember habitually wore a large cross of precious stones – which they were frightened to leave behind in the hut! On their heads were rakish, local plaited straw hats, or even a hibiscus behind the ear.

Those women who disliked going with bare midriffs in front of the Japanese and native soldiers, though it spared material badly needed for patching worn garments, managed some sort of shirt until the end of the war. A popular model was two check dusters, caught at each shoulder, and stitched at the sides, leaving space for armholes, and this was *le dernier cri* with the girls who looked after the pigs. They were unpopular when they returned to barracks, as they stank, but luckily seemed to have fairly extensive wardrobes and looked pretty smart when off duty.

The office staff, following a long tradition of Government offices and departments, grew and waxed fat, and as the Dutch head of the camp was hard-working and conscientious and far too kind-hearted to believe others had not the same high standards as she set herself, she was often misled, and advantage was taken of her kindness. This was particularly so by the woman who volunteered from our group to be head of camp who, though a hard worker, was much disliked. One of the Bandoeng Dutch wrote a book after the war telling of her experiences, and always referred to 'the good Mevr. W., and the bad Mrs S.'.

A job in head office was no sinecure, for there were constant troubles to be settled with both Japanese and women, and with so many different nationalities in the camp, it was impossible to avoid rows and recriminations. Still, whilst some of the staff remained honest and kept high moral standards right through to the end of the war, others did not.

As one of the Japanese officials said: 'Sooner hundred mens than six you women!'

19

Back to the Kitchen

When we first moved to Kampong Makassar most of
the Dutch from Tjideng had paired in friendly cliques,
sharing what they had and living most amicably
together, but as food and conditions worsened, and we
were crowded closer and closer in the barracks, tempers got shorter, and those who had been friends in the
beginning frequently broke away from one another.

Although Corrie and I had dealt out the food from
the beginning, we always found it a worrying, thankless task, and as time wore on it became a never-ending
wrangle, so that we were in danger of becoming nervous wrecks.

The midday meal was bad enough, but as the head
of the hut always dealt out either rice or vegetable
soup, there was not too much argument: when it came
to the evening share-out of bread, which by then had
degenerated into small slabs of rubbery brown dough,
we had to put up with rows night after night. In general
it was admitted we did fairly enough, and most people
in the hut were quite contented we should carry on, for
as soon as someone grumbled we very quickly offered
them the job in our place which they equally rapidly
refused.

As long as women paired, we had been able to put
one small loaf between each two women, leaving it to
them to divide it for themselves, but after a short time
we were asked to divide it for them, and to prevent

further rows in the hut, which were always strident, extremely public and very exhausting to everyone, we did so. Unfortunately we got the bread, as in Tangarang, just before evening roll-call, and had only time to put the tiny half loaves, which had to do two meals, on each place down the hut and hurry out to be in our places in time.

Unless there were sick unable to walk to *appel*, there was no guard in the hut, and people returning from rollcall to our hut, or through it to their own, could, and did, steal.

Consequently, as it was in any case impossible for the sick to do anything, and as more and more women lost their rations, leaving them without food until the following midday unless someone spared them a slice of bread, we had to cut the bread and deal it out after rollcall. All the women were ravenous, and as often as not stood over us whilst we did the dividing.

When the loaves only had to be halved, it was not so bad, but sometimes the bakery was unable to get sufficient tins mended in time, and we were given flat tins of bread which had to be cut up into thirty-three exact portions, each portion being about four by fifteen centimetres, and two or three centimetres high. To do this, the slabs could be divided into two rows of fifteen slices, leaving three slices down one side, and as I had a pretty good eye by that time for dealing out food, I could cut without measuring. Many of the women went at once to get a tape measure to see if I had given a quarter of a centimetre more to somebody else. Fortunately for us, it was usually all right.

When we had the small half loaves to deal out, we put them in a large basket, and dealt them out left and right the whole way up the barracks. Two sisters, who unfortunately slept to one side of me and were always shrilling away about some unfair thing done to them (and sometimes I wondered why it wasn't murder), started to follow us up the hut night after night shouting and scolding that they always got flat bread whilst our friends had risen loaves! As the hut was practically blacked out, and we had neither the chance nor the inclination to sort out special loaves for anybody, Corrie and I got absolutely fed up with the nightly tirade, often joined in by others, equally bad tempered. Finally, we could stand it no longer, and decided to get other work and leave someone else to cope with the division of food.

We were promptly shouted at for being 'no sportsmen', but felt we'd rather bear that than lose our last rags of self-control. I was then warned that if I was to persuade Corrie to do heavy work, she would never stand the strain as she had always been weak, but I felt it was for her to decide, and made up my own mind to join the rice squad, if they would have me.

I had two reasons for choosing this work, for although it was hot, hard and dirty, it was done on alternate nights and at night the camp was moderately peaceful. Also, there had recently been an unholy row in the kitchen because so much food was disappearing and the new head of the kitchen was thoroughly reliable, a part-Chinese who had come from Singapore and was sister to the young woman, Dulcie Nicholas, who had been our head in both Tangarang and Tjideng. Gwen, the older sister, and I had been together since Lengkong, and as she did not get on well with her mother and sister, she'd been glad to come to Makassar.

I was absolutely delighted when she was made the new head of kitchen as she was not only a wonderful worker, but understood a great deal about cooking the food we were given. She was also a very responsible person, and not afraid to say what she thought, when necessary, either to the Japanese or to anyone else.

The trouble over the theft of food was general in all camps in Java, I later discovered, and in Tjimahi, where Charles and the other British and thousands of Dutch were later interned near Bandoeng, the cooking was taken out of the hands of the Europeans and given by the internees to the Chinese, who not only made a better job of it, but did not fatten themselves at the expense of the others.

I didn't imagine that Corrie would be able to stand work on the 'rice-shift', but heard that Gwen needed someone to do her washing and thought this might suit Corrie. Unfortunately Gwen had already fixed it up, so in the end Corrie decided to join the rice squad with me, to give it a trial. Her family were annoyed with me about this, and she undoubtedly did look far too frail for the work, but she could always stop at once if it was too much, and as we worked in pairs, I thought we might try it out.

When the original five hundred women were sent to Kampong Makassar, as I mentioned earlier, there were only five drums for rice squads, cooking on alternate nights, and on average they finished work at about two or three o'clock in the morning, if the fires had burned all right and no rice had been burned. By the time Corrie and I joined, although by then there were well over two thousand, and finally three thousand eight hundred, in Makassar, the total number of drums was never added

to. We therefore had to cook, clean and refill each drum
three times per night to steam enough rice for the
whole camp, even on the poor rations we then had.

I was delighted to find that most of the squad were
girls who had escaped from Singapore, for they were
mostly hard workers, loyal and very easy to get on
with. There were two groups, and ours was led by a
German girl, married to an American who, because of
the unpleasant and difficult time she had had during
internment, became moody and morose. She was a
good leader, though, and we all got on well enough,
though like some of the other Germans who were
interned with us, she was a bit of a bully at times.

One of the best things in our squad was that we all
worked as a team and respected our leader, since as in
any business, the behaviour of the head was copied
right through the whole camp. Then too, by working
through the night we got away for a time from the
degrading fights and squabbles which went on all the
time in the barracks. We were so dead tired after our
shift that on alternate nights we usually slept like logs,
even though the bugs and rats crawled around, and our
space by then was limited to seventy-five centimetres
per person. It was impossible to lie down on one's
back, or turn over without nudging neighbours.

Our first task on starting on the rice squad was to try
to get cigarettes, since it helped such hard work on an
empty tummy to smoke occasionally. We found women
in the Bandoeng group still had tins of English cigarettes, which we hadn't seen for years. All kitchen
workers got an extra half loaf and vegetable soup daily,
so by sparing this, or using it in place of our midday
meal, we were able to barter. Most of the cigarette

owners were shrewd enough to wait until we had started work at night, and were dying for a fag, so that they could drive as hard a bargain as possible. The usual barter was four or five cigarettes for the midday meal portion of food.

As soon as possible after evening rollcall the squad on duty assembled in the kitchen shed, which was almost empty except for one or two cleaners frantically washing the big drums which had been used during the day to cook vegetables. We heaved the drums on to the brick wall over the fire holes, then filled them with water, one third full, which had to be passed from hand to hand in buckets. A wooden steamer covered with hessian was fitted in each drum, and the lid closed.

Wood blocks and faggots, which had been collected during the day and carried from the entrance gate, were brought in from the wood pile and arranged in piles under one of the overhanging roofs, and fires were laid under each drum. We had no paper, and very few matches, so the fires had to be started with bits of bamboo, and lighted from our lighters, which were native ones made from plaited cotton like a long tail inside a metal case which had a flint on top.

When all preparations were made, we went back to eat our evening slices of bread in the hut, and to rest before going on duty.

About nine o'clock, or sometimes much earlier if the wood was wet, or we had to cook with stolen *gedek* – the plaited bamboo with which the stockade was made – because no wood had been brought in, we went to the kitchen shed to start the fires under the drums. Plaited leaf fans were provided for the kitchen, though never enough, and after the wood was alight, we fanned like mad things till the fire began to roar. If the *gedek* was wet, clouds of green, stinging smoke came pouring out of the fire tunnels, and nearly choked and blinded us. One girl worked on the hot-water drum, and five of us on the rice, with three extra women to take turns on the drums, and to help lift the baskets away, and so on.

As soon as the water in the rice drums began to steam, the rice, which in the meantime we had dragged in sacks from the storehouse and washed, was measured and put into each drum, and there was great competition as to whose rice steamed first. We all took turns fanning the fires, which had to be fed and fanned constantly, whether we used wood or *gedek*, and it was a constant worry whether the wood supply could last the night, especially if any fire flamed too high so that the drum became too hot and burned the contents. If the rice was badly burned, it had to be thrown away, and this meant shorter rations for the camp, so one had to be extremely careful not to stoke the fire too quickly.

When the steam rose through the wet rice and started to swell it, we stepped up on to the fire block, took off the huge lid and sprinkled the rice with a quarter of a bucket of boiling water, and then shut the lid again. This had to be done three times, and the third time salt was added to the water – had it been done earlier the rice would not have swelled – and then in another twenty minutes or so the rice was cooked.

Next came the worst job of all, for the fire was now high, and the drum heavy with boiling water and cooked rice sufficient for two hundred and fifty portions. Long bamboo poles were slung through the 'ears' of the drum, and it was lifted to the side of the fire. As there was only a space of at most four feet between each drum, it did not leave much room on the high broken platform for two women on each side to man-oeuvre easily. When it was safely settled at the side of the fire, one woman scooped rice out of the drum into baskets. The steamer was then taken out and the boiling water poured into containers for the diet kitchen, where it was used as a sort of jellied rice water.

After the steamer and hessian had cooled sufficiently to be cleaned, the drum was again filled with cold water, the steamer put back, and the whole lifted once again on to the fire. This process had to be repeated twice more, as each drum had to cook enough rice for seven hundred and fifty portions each night, and be cleaned out thoroughly between each cooking. The sweat rolled down us, and as we had to fan the fires violently much of the time, the smoke choked us and we were black as ink.

Once the first steaming of rice had been put into the baskets and carried through to the rear of the kitchen shed, and the drums re-cleaned and put back on the fires, we were able to relax for a time whilst we waited for the fresh water in the drum to boil. It was during these spare moments that we put an old towel or rag around us over our soaking shirts, and sat on the mud road outside the kitchen to smoke a cigarette. On moonlit nights, the silvery reflections on the long lines of coconut palms standing high over the rows of barracks, and the comparative peace and quietness of the sleeping camp was real balm to our very weary spirits, and all the hard work in the world would not have mattered when we could have a few moments of such peace.

One thing did rather surprise me, and that was that not one of us died of pneumonia, for the night air was frequently cold, and we were invariably soaked with sweat, and kept coming from the frightful heat of the fires and steam of the rice drums to the cool of the mud road outside.

When two drums had been cooked by each person, we were given a plate of cooked rice, which sometimes as a treat was fried in a little oil with some chilli. This meal was greatly depreciated by the rest of the camp, and in fact we had to put up with a good deal of criticism; though when the work became too heavy for us and we asked for volunteers, many who came sneeringly only lasted an hour or two, and none more than one night because the heat or smoke, or both, invariably got them down.

Each drum took roughly two hours, and allowing for cleaning and trouble with one or more drums, or the fires, we were seldom finished before half past four the following morning. Then when the heavy baskets had all been carried through to the serving part of the kitchen, and covered with netting, we made our way wearily back to our huts: there we collected some clean clothes – usually kimonos to sleep in – and soap, if we had it, and went to the wash house to clean ourselves and wash our blackened hair before the rest of the camp woke and poured in.

In principle the rice squad were then allowed to go to the hut and sleep, though the noise of all the others getting up, going to rollcall and having their bread and tea before leaving for work in the gardens was pretty hectic, and not conducive to sleep. However, we did get some rest before going at eleven to the kitchen to help deal out the rice into the baskets belonging to the different huts, which each rice squad had to do on the day following nightshift.

When we first went to Makassar we had been forced to go into the gardens each day to collect what wood we could for the camp, and as this had to be done with wooden or heavy iron handcarts which had been left behind by the soldiers who previously occupied the camp, and which bogged down in the sticky mud in the wet season, many of the women had become ill with the extra work involved. Later, wood was brought in from outside, and though we had to go carefully and there were continual rows between the day and night staff in the kitchen who accused one another of extravagance, we managed fairly well. If no wood had been brought in to the camp by the Japanese, we just stole what we could from the barracks and the inner stockade, which rapidly had large gaps in it. All the same, we hated cooking with *gedek* because of the awful smoke, so that we had to work with bits of wet cloth over our mouths, and, worse still, the rice got smoked.

After the rice for the huts was dealt with, and carried away, we had our meal in the kitchen, and any remains which had been left were divided amongst us, and all other kitchen workers and cleaners. It was these small portions, often very tasty, which we used to bargain for cigarettes, and which caused much hard feeling in the camp.

20
Song and Dance

If I have given the impression that life was so sombre in Kampong Makassar that we thought of nothing but dragging our way through day after day, it is also fair to say that when the food was a little better, or we had some extra sugar from the shop, then people cheered up considerably. We were certainly very much better off than the friends we had left behind in Tjideng.

During one of the brighter periods the girls who looked after the pigs got up a successful cabaret, which was much appreciated. Later, when we were joined by the first Bandoeng camp, Corrie Vonk, a well-known Dutch comedienne, came with them, and put on some very good shows. These were held in a shed with bamboo thatch, supported by poles, a cement floor, and a stage at one end. On three sides it was open, which was an advantage, for in two or three nights the whole camp could see a show.

In any case, many of us preferred to remain outside, if it was in the dry season, as under the roof was too hot and smelly. Many Dutch were fond of perfume, and as a cabaret, or any other show, was an occasion for 'dressing up' – for those who still had something to dress up in – the stifling air simply reeked with scents pleasant and unpleasant.

One great treat was a piano recital given, I think, by a German woman married to a Dutchman. She played beautifully, though the piano the Japanese brought in was very old and rickety and gave her little help. It was a brilliant starry night, and as Corrie and I sat with hundreds of others under the palm trees, which shimmered gently in a light breeze, smoking a last cigarette before going on duty in the kitchen for the night, a feeling of peace crept over the camp, as the lovely music floated out from the bamboo hut.

Another pleasant relaxation came when I met a young Dutch girl whose father, General Schilling, we had known before the war. In fact, he had stayed with us in Soebang with his staff a few weeks before the Japanese invasion, and I had played my last game of golf with him. When we finished, and stood together looking over the lovely little course towards the hills above Bandoeng, he turned to me and said: 'One thing you can be sure of, Mrs Jackson, I shall do my utmost to see that this beautiful place remains as it is.' Three weeks later Soebang was in the hands of the Japanese, and the majority of the staff were either in Bandoeng or other towns – or dead.

Maud Schilling was a delightful girl, and as many people, quite unjustly, blamed on her father the mistakes made when the Japanese invaded Java, I was glad when she moved into our barracks. She had brought several copies of *Studio* into Makassar, and these gave endless pleasure to many people. Looking at all the delightful pictures of exhibitions and paintings was like looking into another world, and did us good.

We also had in the camp a girl of part-Indonesian birth who had studied in England with the Ballet Rambert, who gave us one or two evenings of ballet. I don't remember her name, and have no idea if the dances she did were original, but she had a wonderful sense of rhythm and when she danced there was not a sound from the watching crowd of women.

The most memorable of all her dances was one based on the story of Joan of Arc, for which she wore the usual little black tunic, her legs being bare. She was slim, with a pale olive complexion and finely featured face, from which her black hair swept away and hung round her shoulders.

The first movement of the dance portrayed the early part of Joan's life, as she dreamed and tended her sheep, with a little wooden stick which had a crossbar at one end. In the second movement the rhythm changed, and what had been a shepherd's crook became a sword, and a warlike dance followed. Finally the sword, with its crossed handle, was held aloft and became the cross, and the dance slowed its tempo until finally she stood holding the cross as she was burnt at the stake.

This particular dance made a great impression on many of us, and whilst I watched it I could not help feeling that the dancer had attained perfect rhythm, which to me is the basis of everything.

Amongst the things which helped to make life bearable in camp was a book I'd been lent written by a Czechoslovakian called Martin Kojc. This *Lesson Book of Life* was in Dutch translation, and was probably based on all sorts of religious and philosophical principles, but as it involved relaxation and training one's mind to ignore the present, I found it invaluable in camp, where noise and lack of privacy were the troubles we found hardest to bear.

Kojc suggested that as it was not easy to concentrate

sufficiently at first so that one was not continually brought back by extraneous circumstances (and he little knew how truly he spoke), it was as well to think of some quiet, much loved place or picture, and only after that clear one's mind to a complete blank.

It is a fact that great concentration was at first needed, but after a time it became easier, and such short periods when one could completely eliminate the noise and filth of the camp were of the greatest possible benefit.

In his book Kojc wrote:

If one is objective, then one lives one's life in the present, just as it is, and one feels happy and content. If one is subjective, then one wishes to force a better future, one feels unfortunate, discontented and never attains it. In objectivity lies rest, inner peace, a happy life: in subjectivity, sorrow, unhappiness and need.

Kojc further reminded his readers that they must be peaceful themselves, unselfish and prepared for anything which might happen, and that this life is only one of many, each one giving man a chance to learn more and improve his character. Mental development can only take place when it is wanted, and each sorrow gives one a chance of development. Everyone must go through this life, and it is a question only of what use one makes of one's troubles which is interesting.

As can be imagined, I found this book of Kojc's a great help in camp, and think the principles he suggested sound. In any case, he enabled many of us to accept our difficult life – not in any hopeless way, but by learning to make the best use of what we had.

One other thing was a great help through camp, and later I was to learn that it had been equally effective for

Charles, and that was the thought of the small farm which we had bought in 1936 in south Cornwall. Whenever I was ill, or feeling particularly depressed, I got busy with a pencil and drew plans for the alterations which we wanted to make – the farm was let to tenants whilst we were abroad – or spent my time furnishing the rooms or planning the garden.

I did occasionally wonder whether it had been bombed, but put the thought away, and so I could always retreat to this refuge, and had my moments of greatest contentment when I was there in spirit.

21

Crime and Punishment

In the afternoon when Corrie and I were free from work, we sat in one of the open spaces between the barracks. Java is one of the most fertile, as well as one of the most beautiful, islands in the world. Great flowering trees like Flame of the Forest, Golden Rain, and Amherstia, the orchid tree, grew around Kampong Makassar, so that for the first time for more than two years the Lengkong group could breathe fresh air, and have the space to gaze at lovely surroundings.

Not, alas, for long, for after the arrival of the Bandoeng internees we were once more crowded and bedevilled with the constant noise of women and children.

In their previous camps the Bandoeng groups had used spare clothes and other goods to bargain through holes in the *gedek* stockades with the Indonesians for eggs and other food. When they were brought to Makassar some of them still continued to do this. Eventually several women were caught, and very severely punished by the Japanese, who warned us if anyone else was caught, the whole camp would suffer.

It was difficult to blame those who bargained to get food for their starving children, but many made sales through the *gedek* for sheer bravado, and that seemed indefensible when the whole camp would receive punishment if they were caught.

Eventually three girls were caught by the Japanese,

or maybe given away by the guards, and they were taken to the punishment cell, which was a beastly place, and thoroughly beaten, then left without food or water for a considerable time. Mrs Wetter, the head of the camp, at last managed to get food and blankets to them, for they were only wearing tiny brassières and shorts. Each day they were made to parade like that with the Japanese taking rollcall, wearing placards saying why they had been punished. Their heads were shaved, and they were not allowed to cover them. It was a horrible punishment, and they were badly bruised, and though we did not have much sympathy with some of the *gedekkers* we were thankful when the punishment ended.

In Tjideng the same beating and punishment had been carried out when the older boys were caught with women who, it must be said, in many cases seduced them, and they too had to walk the camp with shaven heads and placards to say why they were punished.

After the punishment of the women in Kampong Makassar, the Japanese were out for blood, and one day swooped down on barrack No. 14, which was on the outer perimeter of the camp, and rounded up about ten women, some of whom had never disobeyed a rule in their lives. They were all taken away to the punishment cell, and later had their heads shaved on the parade ground. By this time it had become obvious from the news which leaked in through the hospitals and elsewhere that the war must be coming to an end. The ten poor women were most upset because if their husbands were still alive – and they mostly had no idea whether they were or not – then besides looking haggard skeletons or swollen almost out of recognition they would now have to meet them with sheared heads.

Many internees, including children, were ill by July, 1945, and though a few of the worst cases were sent off to Batavia hospitals, most were taken to our own hospital hut. It was by then packed full, with women and children lying on the usual bamboo platforms each side of the hut, but no beds, so the task of the voluntary nurses was made doubly difficult.

Since it was impossible to reach a patient to lift or wash her as she lay at right-angles to the pathway, when a woman was obviously dying she had to be put sideways along the edge of the platform, so that she could be more easily handled.

Corrie's mother, who had now heard for certain that her husband had died, was daily growing weaker, and though the news was probably no surprise to her, and she bore the shock most bravely, we were afraid she too would die. She was supposed to be on a strict fruit diet, but this was like asking for the moon, though Hennie did manage occasionally to steal a papaya on her way back from working in the piggeries.

Amongst the last group to come to Makassar was a young girl who had gone mad, and for some days she was put in a tiny hut, since there was no other place for such a patient. For several days those who lived in the hut nearest to her shed were much upset whenever it rained by the poor demented girl hanging half out of the small window, shrieking and tearing her hair. At last she was removed – God knows where to – but not before the whole camp was on edge.

From the end of May we had blackouts, which made

our own job in the kitchen infinitely more difficult and dangerous. Going over the deep trenches by the slippery bamboo bridges in the dark was bad enough, but when the Japanese suddenly appeared, shouting and cursing at us, we were all terrified to go or come back from the kitchen at night.

Sometimes just after we had reached the shed and got the fires going, the air raid alarm sounded. All fires had to be doused at once, whilst we were ordered to go and sit in another shed. The Japanese who came into the kitchen were in such a state that they cursed and swore because the fires were not damped down, and chucked buckets of water over everything. Sometimes the rice in the drums was already steaming, and this was of course spoiled and wasted.

Worse followed, for when we were allowed back in the kitchen to restart the process, the fire holes were filled with water, and the wood was soaking, so that it took ages even to get the fires burning smokily again, and everything was hours delayed. On such nights we seldom finished in time to get any rest, but had to wash and go back at once to the kitchen to help with the dealing and serving of food.

Deaths rose sharply once more, and it was at that moment when we were all in a highly overwrought state that we were ordered to remain for punishment and prayer in our barracks for two days without food or water.

We supposed that things were going badly for the Japanese, but did not know then that the bombing of Japan was being carried out.

On the day we were ordered to remain in our huts without food, no adequate reason was given, but we accepted the situation as philosophically as we could, and indeed many of the women were only too thankful to get a rest from the heavy work in the vegetable gardens and elsewhere.

At first we were forbidden to leave the huts at all, but as the Japanese were always terrified of epidemics, and we all had dysentery, we were later given permission to go to the latrines, but not to the bath sheds.

A few weeks previously an order had been posted that women in each barracks were to catch flies and take them to the Japanese office each morning. We all sat on our platforms with some sort of fly swat and usually sent several hundreds from each hut every day – the filthiest job was that they all had to be counted before handing in.

The first punishment day some women still had a slice or two of their previous day's bread ration, and some even tinned food, and so were able to get through all right, but the majority of us had only a little peanut butter, which we stamped and made ourselves, and a few scraps of bread.

We rested, read or gossiped fairly peaceably, but by afternoon everyone was hot and cross, and the children, though there were relatively few with us as the original five hundred workers had been kept together, were lying listlessly on their pallets. After all the years of insecurity, bad conditions and noise, we were most of us too tired to care any more what happened, and just hoped to stay alive from day to day.

We vaguely knew that the war in Europe had ended, for news of this got through from a hospital, but things had gone on for so long that we felt we had been abandoned, and so long as we could keep going from day to day, we had little thought to spare for what was happening in the outside world, or even for our families. Survival was all that mattered, and we hung on desperately reserving what little strength we had for the daily work.

For this reason, although in some ways we were all glad of an enforced rest, we felt the cessation of work to be a bad thing, for it gave us time to think, and also to realize how hungry we were. Of course the British group had been more or less hungry for nearly three years, and to a certain extent had got used to it, but it was just when one was forced into inactivity that it became so hard to bear, which was why so many of us preferred to work.

There were, however, exceptions to this, and the Frenchwomen who were brought late into Kampong Makassar were a case in point. When they first arrived, they had done some of the work, as being the only way to get extra food, but they soon decided that the work was far too heavy, and refused to do any, preferring to go without the pay which for the rest of us helped to make life a little more bearable. It was quite a sight to go into their hut, for in the morning the majority of them would be sitting on their bamboo platforms busy with needlework, altering clothes, etc., and almost without exception they had cosmetics and were carefully made up. How they managed to keep supplies going even outside camp I do not know, but it was an inspiring sight, and they were a pleasure to look at. All the same, the work of the camp had to be done whether one liked it or not, since that was why we were sent there, and the less some worked, the more fell on the backs of the others.

By the end of the first day of punishment few people had anything to eat, or if they had they dared not bring it out in the face of so many hungry internees. All through the long, hot night women and children turned and tossed in misery on the hard platforms, their stomachs aching and gnawing for lack of food. The second day dawned, and the only people who moved were those who had to try to drag themselves to the latrines.

During the afternoon one of the Japanese in charge of the pigs appeared secretly at one side of the barracks and handed in some green papayas for the children. He had always been quite a decent little chap, and had often allowed the girls who worked under him to take food which had been brought for the pigs. At any rate, he shut his eyes to a great deal which went on, so that squad worked more cheerfully and happily than any other which was in direct contact with the Japanese.

The Japanese have a name for being kind to children, and it is true that during the three years I was interned I occasionally saw some playing and giving presents to interned children, and teaching them games and wrestling. I also saw them quite unmoved in the hospitals where pitiful sick children lay with arms and legs like little sticks, and bodies and faces swollen out of all recognition by malnutrition. The squads of small children in the vegetable gardens had worked the same as their mothers, and they suffered just the same punishments and starvation as we did, so that many of them died or were sick for years afterwards.

It may be that the orders to starve the internees came from higher up, but the Japanese is a martyr to discipline, and would never question any order given to him, but would obey it whatever his personal feelings.

On the evening of the second day's punishment, those of us who worked on the rice squad were suddenly ordered to turn out, and when we got to the kitchen we had to carry out and then cook nearly double the usual amount of rice.

The extra drums to cook this sudden large quantity of food were, needless to say, not provided, so we had to work all night on empty stomachs, cooking the rice. About half-way through the night we were able to get our first meal, when part of the rice had been cooked, and after forty-eight hours with only snacks of food, some of the girls were sick.

Because we were slower than usual, and the wood did not burn as it had been stacked out in the rain and not under the kitchen roof, we did not finish the rice cooking until after eight the following morning – about thirteen hours' work.

The squad were simply wonderful, and all managed to get their portions cooked, though by morning we were all absolutely exhausted and thankful to get off duty.

22

The Sick and Dying

By the end of June, 1945, of the three thousand eight
hundred who were still interned in Kampong Makassar, including the original five hundred, many had
been taken to hospital in Batavia when our own barracks hospital became too full.

Some mothers had consistently starved themselves
to try to feed their children. It was understandable, but
made things very difficult when they became seriously
ill, or died, as a result. Others had then to take over
responsibility for the children as well as their own
work. About thirty wives of our Company staff were
then in Makassar, some very ill.

Fortunately I was able to borrow quite a large sum of
money from Corrie's sister, Hennie, to be paid back in
Dutch guilders after the war, but without interest. This
was most unusual, for in some cases as much as three
hundred per cent was asked, and signed for, though
objections sometimes came when the loan had to be
repaid after the war. The money was absolutely invaluable at that time in saving lives, and in that way no
price was too high to pay. It also had to be remembered
that not everyone was in the employ of a large Company – and even then my husband had a hard task after
the war insisting that the money he had been able to
borrow to keep staff alive was a debt of honour and
must be repaid at the rate asked. Such money was
sometimes the only source of income for the internee

lender after the war, unless conditions enabled jobs to be obtained in Java, which seemed unlikely.

Still, a great deal of profiteering did go on, and not only over money. Sick patients in hospitals had their few remaining clothes stolen, and jewels, money and other possessions often disappeared as they lay dying. A priest hacked out the gold fillings from a dead man's mouth, and yet another patient, as he lay dying, was heard to say to the nurse who was stealing the money from under his pillow, 'You might at least wait until I'm dead.'

As soon as I got the money from Hennie I was able to send some to desperately sick Company wives in a Batavia hospital. Unfortunately I sent the money through the office, giving the name and number of women concerned to Summerskill. Two weeks later I got an urgent message begging for money for necessities for one of the wives, then desperately ill, and only then did I find her money had been given to someone else, who had signed for it and used it.

During the last months in camp there was a great deal of trouble between nationalities, and by July the tension was so great that the Japanese moved the British and foreign nationals into the last barracks, No. 14, to separate them from the Dutch.

It was generally expected in Makassar, as elsewhere in Java, that the Americans would come and release us, and many of us – not only the British – were fed up with the attitude taken by some internees who belittled anything which the British had done, saying it was fortunate there were Americans to get us out of the mess. Much as I longed for the British to arrive, I rather hoped, in view of the dreadful job which any Army was going to have clearing things up both in Java and the islands, that it would be the Americans who came.

Shortly after our move to No. 14 barracks, I had a feeling I should soon stop working with the rice squad, and took it to mean that the war must be over. Unfortunately, instead of that I got mumps, and was horrified to think Charles might first see me after three and a half years with a face resembling a full moon. Like· all epidemics, it ran through the camp, and because of the cold winds and endless trips to the latrines, it was hard to cure. Corrie had left the rice squad when I did, and despite bitter opposition, came to visit me. She remained a most loyal friend, and I was glad to have the chance to help her later.

Some of us were absolutely delighted to notice at this time that the bamboo supports of the huts were being eaten away by white ants, since the Indonesians believe that this signifies a move. Not all the women were so rapturous, though, when they found that in a single night the ants could, and did, eat their way through whole leather suitcases and their contents!

A few weeks previously we had been worried when twice within a short space of time we were ordered to take what luggage we could carry out to the parade ground, where it was picked over by the guard and inspected, after which we were closely watched as we carried it away. Surprisingly, some people still had several large cases and chests, under which they tottered. If they had only felt able to share a little of what they still had, others would have been glad to help them carry the rest. Even at this late date, some women hoarded like misers, and one woman died of starvation with food which would have saved her life still intact in her case.

We heard after that the practice moves we had carried out were in preparation for sending us to work in the ricefields of Borneo. If that is so, I can only say that very few indeed would have survived such a trip, let alone with the prospect of coolie work at the end of it.

—

23

The End of the War

I don't ever recollect being told by the Japanese that the war was over and that Japan had capitulated, though for the last few weeks their behaviour varied according to whether they had been harsh or not. The kinder ones told the girls working with the pigs that they need no longer work so hard, as soon they would be outside the barbed wire and the Japanese behind it, whilst the bad ones were more brutal than ever. Colonel Sonè came into the last category.

By August we knew the war really was ending, but by that time we were so tired, and the sights we had seen and the life we had lived had been so dreadful, that we hardly dared to believe the rumours, and just staggered on from day to day.

When the news came officially, at first everyone was just stunned and apathetic, but gradually as better food was poured in and Red Cross parcels were distributed, the spirits of the camp rose.

Because of the change-over from American to British control for this area of South East Asia, there had to be a time lag of about six weeks before the occupation troops could arrive from Malaya. Although that country was retaken without fighting, it naturally took time for the Forces to be reorganized for Java, and though this could not possibly have been avoided, it did put us in a rather curious position. We were still guarded by a few Japanese, and had to remain in our camps and prisons.

Many of the women who had lived in Batavia broke camp, some going through a very bad time when they reached the town, and one or two being stoned outside the camp by angry Indonesians, and told to get back behind the barbed wire.

It has been said and written that prior to the Japanese invasion there was no anti-Dutch feeling in Java or elsewhere, but I do not think this was so. For many years there had been small groups of agitators, working in a Nationalist movement, but they may have been a small minority.

Many Dutch not unnaturally felt bitter when they were not allowed out of the camps to start the various services running again on the island, but the situation was such that unless the whole of Java could be controlled at once, which was manifestly impossible because of all the sickness and lack of enough Europeans, the thousands of Dutch women and children gathered together into the internment camps could all have been massacred.

For the first week or so after the capitulation of Japan we had five or six Japanese left to guard the camp, and as the British and other foreigners were in No. 14 barracks, which was only protected by a barbed wire fence as most of the *bilik* stockades had by then been burnt for firewood, we were the nearest to contact with the outside world.

One night after lights-out – and in a way life and work continued as if nothing had happened – a drum was heard from the native village which lay a short distance below the vegetable gardens. More drums joined in, and soon there was a terrific noise – a frightening enough sound at any time – and a feeling of tension could plainly be felt running through the occupants of the barracks.

Peeping through the air vents we had cut in the bamboo walls, processions of torches we could see in the velvety darkness making their way to a central meeting point, where the tom-toms continued with ever-increasing fervour, accompanied by shouts and yells. Speeches and intermittent shouting, aided by the beating of the drums, went on for a time, till finally there was a pause – and the screaming, shouting mob began to move into the gardens, and the drumming became frenzied.

By this time the fear of every woman and child in the barracks could be actively felt, as we waited in terror for the natives to rush the barbed wire and then murder the lot of us.

The few guards on the camp had to cover about six kilometres of wire, and if they wanted to see us finished off, now was their chance. Just as our hearts were in our mouths as the drumming and screeching reached a crescendo, sheets of rain began to fall like a cloudburst, the drumming gradually slowed and died away till finally, except for the hammering of the rain, there was silence.

It was a most terrifying experience, and few of us slept that night.

Shortly after this, about seventy-five Dutchmen were sent to the camp from internment nearby, to help with the hard work, and twelve RAF moved into the head office. These men had been POWs since 1942, and at least two had been with 84 Squadron in Soebang, so when I heard of their arrival I was delighted, and we welcomed one another like long-lost friends.

Amongst the Dutch helpers were the husbands of some of our internees, and though many did marvellous work in the camp, a few sat around with their wives, which got on the nerves of the women who now knew of their husband's death or still anxiously awaited news. Of course the husbands and wives wanted to be together, but they might have been more tactful in their behaviour, and in any case even the most thoughtless person should have been pulled up by the sight of the hundreds of weeping women in the barracks.

Another difficulty was that after being parted for some years, some wives had decided not to renew a marriage which had been unhappy, or had found someone else to love in the intervening years. In such cases, it was not infrequent for husbands to come to the stockade door asking for their wives, only to be sent a message that the wife refused to come. When children were also involved, the saddest situations arose, with people crying both inside and outside the camp.

It was the painful work of Mrs Wetter – Mrs Simington had left to work in a Batavia hotel, where she had also managed a job for her husband, and this despite the fact she had herself asked to be head of the camp – and Mr Young (the RAF ex-POW now in charge of Kampong Makassar) to deal with these and many other dreadful situations, and they worked wonderfully together.

The British, too, had reason to be grateful to Mr Young for all his help and encouragement, and I hope one day he will read this account and realize what his kindness meant to us.

Shortly after Mr Young's arrival, our hut leader, whose husband had died, wanted to get to Batavia to work in the hospital, and I took over as head of the barracks.

There was a great deal to do, finding out where people wanted to go, and helping with arrangements for them and their families.

At last Charles was able to send me a letter – he really was alive! – and I learned that he and Mr Crichton – the Consular official who stayed behind and did fine work during the internment of the men – had been chosen to come to Batavia and inspect all the women's camps, so that they could report back on the conditions, and make plans for removing the women.

When I got the letter I rushed to tell Corrie, but told her too that with the work my husband had taken on, I should be lucky if I saw him for half an hour!

In the meantime the work of the camp had to be continued, and as many of the women in the work squad had refused to do any more work when the war ended, had it not been for volunteers doing double work, the camp would have been a stinking cesspool in no time. Some actually refused to work because, they said, their husbands had senior positions, so it would not be right for them to work. This struck me as just as funny as the Government officials first interned with the British in Soeka Miskin, who at an arranged hour were called upon in their cells by their junior officials – suitably dressed, of course!

That such a thing should happen at the beginning of internment was bad enough, but that some of the wives should still have the same pretentious ideas to which they returned hot-foot after years of hell, shows we either hadn't been interned long enough or that some women were apparently unteachable.

I was so happy to have letters from Charles, and to know that I should shortly see him, even for a few moments, that I found it hard not to go round the camp singing and shouting, but I was sobered quickly enough by the thin, sad faces round me.

On 13 September (my lucky number) just a week after our sixteenth wedding anniversary, Charles arrived in camp about eleven o'clock with Mr Crichton. He was painfully thin, but being sunburnt and in fairly good clothes borrowed from friends for the trip, he did not look too bad. In fact, we neither of us cared about our looks because we were together again.

Mr Crichton, bless his heart, went to interview some of the internees, and find out their plans, whilst Charles and I quickly compared notes and letters, and then hurriedly made some plans. After that, the two men saw other British wives, and then left for the next camp.

They had five other camps and hospitals to visit, and though Charles did say he would try to get out once again before he left for Bandoeng – he was staying two nights at the hotel with a Japanese guard! – I knew there was little chance of it.

As a matter of fact, I tried to swing the lead and get him to let me stay at the hotel too, but I should have been disappointed if he had agreed to it, and, needless to say, I hadn't a hope.

When he got back, Charles sent me word that he was trying to get Company wives and children moved to

Bandoeng as soon as possible, but that it was extremely difficult to find accommodation. He did what he could from Tjimahi to get things going, and told me to stay where I was and look after things my end as best I could. I hated being parted from him, but as usual he was quite right, and there was a great deal to be arranged.

The fact that it was the British who were coming to Java had been very badly received by many of the internees, though two Americans married to Dutchmen were fine, and got to work to help as fast as they could.

One reason for anger was that it was not understood why the women could not be moved at once, and join their husbands where possible, since many refused to believe how bad the situation outside the camps really was. Altogether, it was a horrible mess, and if our tempers were short, there was usually a reason for it.

24
Visits

In the beginning of September, 1945, I had my first
cable from home, through the Red Cross, saying all the
family had survived the war, and Jane was happy in
Australia. From that date we were able to send letters
and cables intermittently, and I could try occasionally
to telephone Charles in Bandoeng on a very bad line.
The courier service between Bandoeng and Batavia
camps was invaluable, and I got letters fairly regularly.

There was a great feeling of sadness over the camp, for
at last many of the women had heard for certain news of
their husbands, and many had died in the camps. I felt
ashamed at times for being so happy in the face of so
much sorrow, and had many sad moments sitting with
wives of the Company staff who had received bad news,
or, what was really worse, no news at all.

Cables started arriving from Holland, and when news
came through of all that had happened there, and of
the numbers killed or missing following the German
occupation, there was little happiness in Kampong
Makassar. I got extra home news through letters from
Charles, as when he returned to Tjimahi he found that
one of the Britishers had managed to get a wireless in
Bandoeng, and had installed it in their room, enabling
the British at last to get some news from home.

The Red Cross sent in a case of books, so that we
were able to read something about the story of the war,
of which we knew practically nothing.

We were often joined in the mud compound outside our hut in the evenings by some of the RAF men who were on the outside staff, and they then passed on to us what they had learned during the day. In such a manner we listened fascinated to stories of the main battles, inventions and discoveries of the war. These narratives were just as wonderful to the POWs as they were to us, so we sat like children night after night round a charcoal fire, sometimes cooking up a meal of eggs or whatever we had managed to save for the men, who were always hungry.

We loved these restful hours when we'd all done a hard day's work, and I think the men enjoyed them too, for they too were feeling out of touch with the world, just as we were, and were perhaps glad to talk to women before getting back to their homes. Unfortunately, however, some of the Dutchwomen complained to Mr Young, who joined us himself when he could, and what had been a most innocent and happy relaxation had to be ended through jealousy.

My first letter to my husband after his return to Bandoeng was dated 17 September, and mentions that once we were discovered by the Cycle Camp – the Forces camp nearest to us – we were inundated with visitors. Forty-three of 84 Squadron were still alive, and many of them popped in and out. One pet of a Cockney, who looked like Laurel, of Laurel and Hardy fame, when he was finally dragged from the barracks, put his head back through the door, saying 'Expect me at midnight, girls,' which made us feel almost human again.

Corrie came in one afternoon, after trying to get to see her mother who was extremely ill in St Vincentius hospital, after news confirming her husband's death in Ambarawa. He'd apparently done marvellous work with secret radio, and spent two years with the *Kempei*. By great luck, a man from 84 was in the office with Mr Young, and lent his car for Corrie and Hennie to get to Batavia.

I still had to work on the night shift of the rice squad, as it was short handed, but got little rest during the day with so many callers. One group from the Cycle Camp had sent us fruit, and then fl.100 each in case we were short, followed by a further visit bringing eggs, fruit, half a sack of sugar, and other presents. These included a set of undies (vest and pants) stitched in large blue stitching and made from coarse Japanese material.

I wrote to Charles:

They are all darlings, and look after us like nobody's business. The rest of the camp is mad with jealousy, but we just don't care any longer. These boys, I've heard incidentally, sold their clothes to get money, etc. for us, and when I taxed one of them with it, he looked frightfully embarrassed and said it was only Nippon clothes. He added, proudly fingering his British Army shirt, 'But we get much more for these, you know!' What pets they are.

One afternoon when we were told to expect the RAF padre, Mrs Wetter suddenly appeared at our barracks with a tall man in glasses, wearing a navy tammy. This was Colonel Dewar, the British officer in charge sent by SEAC. Other officers turned up shortly, including Major Greenhalgh, who was parachuted into Java first, and Mr Young. Only then did we realize who Colonel Dewar was. He had been right through the war, and looked a mass of nerves under tight control, until Mrs

Wetter asked why things didn't happen quicker. I thought he would let fly, but he said: 'The British have been left with the dirty end of the stick as usual, and we have two million people to return or move. We expected that Java etc. would be taken care of by MacArthur, but now we must do that too, and I am here as a sort of Government and heaven knows what, with a staff of fifteen men. We have lost a tremendous amount of shipping, but you are not the last on the list, though Java has not suffered so badly – Sumatra and Celebes come after you!' Then later, when he was still very angry, because Mrs Wetter tried to tell of the bad time we'd had, he said: 'I've just come from Germany where people are lying ten deep in the streets, and where in one camp alone ten thousand men are lying dying.' He told us he'd been through the whole show – Dunkirk, Norway, Libya, etc. – for six years, and he ended: 'We don't want the Dutch East Indies, we don't want anything, we've got enough of our own. All we want is to get home, so you see things will be done as fast as possible. In the meantime we'll try to free those who can go, bring husbands and wives together – possibly in camps temporarily – but the problem in each country is not the Nips, who are trying for whatever reason to be as helpful as possible, but the Nationalist question, and that is a Big Trouble.'

Life continued as usual after that, until our next excitement. HMS *Cumberland* was in port, and Rear Admiral Patterson was visiting us after the Cycle Camp. He was, I heard, delighted at morale, but horrified by the conditions in the women's camps, and invited all the British women aboard his ship for a day's outing.

Many years later my description of that was:

On the Sunday morning a group of (British) women and children from each camp piled into buses for their first free drive through the town since internment.

We drove through Batavia, horribly dilapidated and dirty. Gardens choked with weeds, streets filled with beggars with only a few rags to cover themselves, and indescribably filthy. To those of us who remembered the pleasant houses and gardens before the war, the change was horrifying.

However, we were quickly through the town, and were on holiday, so we sang as we drove along, and the little children could hardly keep still as they squealed at first one excitement and then another. Many of them remembered nothing but their life in the camps, and to drive in a bus, and see cars and soldiers and – finally – the sea and ships, was almost too much for them.

Nearly all of us had saved a dress of some sort 'for the day we leave camp'. With the aid of a charcoal iron which we used on the flat ground outside our hut to press our clothes, we really did look an amazingly neat, if not smart, collection of women and children.

Most of us had short hair, which we took turns to cut for one another, and though it had been impossible to get rid of the red dust of the camp, nevertheless we felt we had done our best not to look too much like 'poor bloody internees'.

Before we went on board, the children caught sight of the loaves of white bread which could be seen through an open scuttle, and their eyes simply goggled. From then on they had the day of their lives. We went on board, and after shaking hands with the Admiral and officers, each child was given into the care of a sailor who would look after him for the rest of the day, leaving mothers free to rest, meet friends from other camps, or go over the ship.

The hospitality was wonderful, and we were showered with gifts. I've never seen such kind people in my life – and instead of enjoying myself I sat in a corner and howled, as did many other women. It was just too much for us after all the horror and misery of the past three-and-a-half years.

After a bit I felt better, and was glad of the chance to find out about friends I'd left behind in other camps, many of whom were too ill to come.

We were given a wonderful lunch on board, and then some of the young people were dying to dance again. As they were a little shy of starting, I found myself to my amazement leading off with the padre!

Alas, such happiness had to come to an end. The most dreadful time followed, for the children wept and begged to be allowed to stay on board with the sailors, and many of the sailors themselves had tears in their eyes.

Finally, we had to return before dusk to our horrible camps, but we were grateful from the bottom of our hearts for the truly wonderful day we had been given. I doubt if anyone on the ship had any toothbrush, paste, soap, or a thousand other necessities, not to mention the sugar which the whole ship's company went without so that the camps might benefit.

After thirty-one years the memory of that day still makes me cry.

After this visit, arrangements went ahead to try to get those who were not sick out of the camps. Mr Young and another RAF man, Dick Crissop, volunteered to stay on till we got fixed up, after which they would be flown direct home. All other POWs were taken off by Sunderlands within a few days.

Though my husband and I had little time for our own affairs, one thought was firmly in our minds, and that was that by hook or by crook we would be 'Home for Christmas'.

25
Goodbye Java

By the end of September, I found I could not do anything further at the Batavia end, and decided to leave the camp and fly to Bandoeng to join Charles.

Before going, I managed to scrounge a lift to Tjideng, still in an appalling state despite help from the Navy and others, where I saw Emmy Starkey and her husband, who had decided not to fly to Singapore with most of the other British. I had hoped to see Deborah and Ferne, but found she had been moved to a large hotel being used as a hospital, and with a bit of luck got a lift there.

Deborah had by then been joined by her husband, Noel, and though she was still extremely ill and unable to fly to Australia, she put on her usual cheerful act, and it was lovely to see her and Ferne and Noel all together again.

I tried to get a phone call put through to Charles to say I was hoping to fly the following day, but there was the usual mess-up, and after waiting some time in terrible weather, he returned to his camp, leaving a note for me at a hotel. Luckily I met a man from RAPWI, the organization for repatriating internees, and he took me to the address I'd been given by the van Galen Lasts.

As always, they made me welcome, but there was terrible fighting and looting in the town. At the moment the Indonesians were more friendly with the British than the Dutch, so I hoped I might be a help to Gerrit and Ita in case they too were raided.

The next three weeks were a nightmare: looting, murdering and burning of houses at night which in one way made it the most frightening time of the whole Japanese occupation. Charles and I left before the end of October, but the Dutch had to suffer many, many months of such terror, and it was small wonder that in the end their patience failed, and that they complained of the lack of understanding with which the situation was handled.

The majority of the British who came over with the Army had already fought a long, hard war, and were quite naturally fed up with the idea of having to stay on to clear up a mess which had nothing to do with them, with the result that there was not always good co-operation on either side, and the best certainly was not made of men who had lived in the country for years, and who understood the situation fairly well, and how it could best be handled.

I do not mean the political situation, for the British did not intend to interfere there, but certainly more use could have been made of both Dutch and British planters and others who offered their services and were – sometimes very rudely – told that they could not be used.

The looting by British troops also caused very bad feeling, and did a great deal of harm.

One of the saddest things was the bad feeling caused when officers and men who came over to Java took mistresses. These were often women who were known to have been living with Japanese, and who now hoped to escape retribution. This was almost bound to happen when men who had been living in many cases through hell for the past few years were not allowed to return to their families, and the Dutch themselves were far from faultless, but it added to all the other difficulties.

Because Charles and I were exceptionally lucky, and were able to stay with kindly friends and live a relatively normal life in a house, it is impossible for me to criticize, but it saddened me that many of the tragedies which arose out of the period of enforced separation had enormous after-effects, as they did in other parts of the world. Many of the men and women who rushed into hasty affairs at that time had bitter cause to regret their behaviour later, when a good marriage broke up as a result.

For the first few days in Bandoeng I saw little of Charles, since when he was not in town seeing a mass of officials and others, he was back clearing things up with Company staff in Tjimahi. Finally he did arrive in Bandoeng, but by that time he had tired himself out, and for the next three days and nights he had a high fever. While I sat by his bed, he raved and rambled about many of the terrible things which had happened over the past years, but at last the fever left him, and he was able in a few days to get about again, though he was pitifully thin.

Gerrit and Ita had managed to get back a house, and even a little of their furniture, and some of their servants had rushed back to them also, just as ours were to do when we later returned to Java. The servants had many tales to tell of the dreadful time under the Japanese, but sadly after a week or so most Indonesians were far too frightened by the extremists to do any work for Europeans.

—

Terrible scenes happened daily and nightly, and each time Charles or Gerrit had to leave the bungalow, we waited in fear until they returned. Shooting happened nightly, and it is small wonder that many people who had managed to survive the horrible camps now broke down under new terrors, and that they begged for protection and help.

There were not nearly enough British troops to keep order, which was hardly surprising considering the enormous job which had been suddenly pushed on to them. The whole situation was made appallingly difficult by the huge crowds of women and children still held in camps in Java, who had to be safeguarded because it was not possible for them to return to their homes, many of which had been destroyed. Finally, when Charles felt there was nothing more he could do, we at last made arrangements to fly to Batavia and try to leave for Singapore. At last we said goodbye to Gerrit and Ita, who were such wonderful friends, and though we were sad to leave them, the last few days had been increasingly difficult, for the Dutch did not like at all the way things were being handled in Java, and each night as we listened to speeches on the wireless, our friends had grown more restive, so that we felt we should leave.*

Charles and I got a bus to the Airport, and after weighing in our one little attaché case, stepped on to the plane, only to find we had a Japanese pilot.

Well, I certainly thought that would be the end of us,

* For a description of the following tragic year, and the murder of General Mallaby, see Chapters 21–25 of *The Fighting Cock*: The story of the 23rd Indian Division by Lt.-Col. A. J. F. Doulton, OBE.

but apart from a few bugs in the wicker chairs, it was one of the best flights I ever had.

Things were absolutely chaotic in Batavia, and as dangerous as Bandoeng. No flight was possible, until by the greatest of good luck as we despondently left the RAPWI building I felt a hand on my arm, and saw the delighted face of Dick Crissop.

He and Mr Young were working in Batavia, and leaving for home shortly. In no time they had got passages for us on a Singapore flight the following day, and fixed some sort of accommodation in an absolutely packed-out little Indonesian hotel. How we did bless them!

At crack of dawn we thankfully left behind the noise and shooting of Batavia, and boarded the plane.

26

Hello Australia

After an excellent flight to Singapore, and a kindly welcome, we were back once more in crowded conditions at Sea View Hotel amongst many of the people we had thought we would not have to see again, in the huge RAPWI camp.

We knew we might have to wait days, maybe weeks, before we could get away to Australia to collect Jane, but standing again in queues for baths and food, and seeing once again people grabbing all they could get was a bit too much. Hiring a cheerful little Chinese taxi-man for a week, we fled to Raffles Hotel, which was still requisitioned, and away from the streaming hordes of refugees.

Luckily the hotel was beginning to take guests, and we managed to get a room. Absolute heaven, and with a very good Chinese servant in attendance, we got our few clothes washed quickly, a necessity as we could not spare a set for long. We rushed around pulling plugs and running water to our heart's content, and were at last able to send cables, get some money and other necessities.

During the period of waiting to get on a plane or ship, we were joined by Hank Quade, an American friend from camp who later became our son Simon's godfather, who took us with him when visiting Chinese friends. Many other friends turned up, and we heard that some of the men from the Company who had been on the notorious Railway were in camp in Singapore, and hoping to see Charles.

One story touched me very much. Gwennie Williams, a young wife of only three weeks who had got out of Singapore to Java at the last moment, and had been with me in Lengkong and other camps, had returned to Singapore. She had heard no word from her husband, and presumed he must have been killed – he was in the Army. One morning as she sadly went down to breakfast in Raffles Hotel, then used for refugees, she pushed the dining-room door at the same moment someone pushed from the other side. It was her husband. He had been desperately ill in Borneo, and sent back to Singapore, where he could get no news of his wife. It was lovely to think that after all Gwennie's courage, her story had such a happy ending.

When we got to the camp where some Dutch members of the Company were waiting, they were delighted to see Charles, and longing to return to work, though he had to explain that there was small chance of that at present. Some had already been offered jobs on Malayan rubber estates, and were anxious to get their families over from the awful camps. My husband promised to do what he could, and we went off happy to think that at least some of the many women who had waited so anxiously for news might at last be able to join their husbands.

Our happiness was short-lived. The British we saw next day were polite and agreed at once that permits would be granted the wives immediately, provided that some accommodation was arranged. The Dutch authorities, after keeping us waiting literally hours, absolutely refused to give permission to the wives, explaining that if one woman was allowed to come, hundreds of others would want to follow. One would have thought this would be a good idea, but this was not the attitude taken, though at last Charles did get permission for one or two wives.

Although we had great difficulty in getting any sort of passage, at last on 3 November we were collected with other internees in a jeep, and driven at break-neck speed – with the driver keeping up a cheery conversation all the way – down to the dock. I was put in a cabin with five other women, and Charles with five men, when we got on board. In fact we were lucky, as the ship was absolutely crammed with troops and nurses being taken back to Australia – carefully segregated, of course – and most of the men had a wretched journey down in the hold.

Although the journey to Australia was not a particularly pleasant one, the main thing was we were on our way home, even if that did include a detour to Australia en route. It was impossible to radio Australia, as no British ships were allowed to do so, but after a voyage via Balik Papan and the Lombok Straits, we finally docked at Fremantle.

We did not really expect to see Jane there to meet us, since we had not been able to let her know when we would be arriving, but nevertheless we hung over the rail anxiously as the boat moved slowly in, scanning the huge crowd down on the quay. Suddenly, there she was, a long-legged child in school uniform and black stockings, and with her was our old friend Titus Miller.

Jane had grown tremendously, and looked beautifully

sunburnt and well. Nell and Titus had looked after her marvellously through the four years, and had sent her to an excellent school, the only one which did not evacuate from Perth when a Japanese invasion seemed imminent. As a result the Presbyterian Ladies College had grown from about a hundred and eighty to six hundred pupils, and well deserved its success.

Accommodation was difficult, but for a night we were in the same hotel as dear Deborah, Ferne and Noel, and it was wonderful to see her out of hospital and on the slow way to recovery.

Perth is a fine town, and from our own experience there it is filled with the kindest, most hospitable people, who went out of their way to do all they could for us, just as they had shown great kindness to the many children who had arrived there as evacuees and lived there during the war.

We settled into a room at the Palace Hotel, and Jane returned to school to finish her term, seeing us each weekend. She had enjoyed her years at PLC, and had made friends with a delightful family, the Vincents, who were to remain lifelong friends. Both Charles and I badly needed to see a dentist, whilst we waited hopefully for a plane home, and it was urgently necessary for Charles to see a doctor, as ever since his beatings by the *Kempei* his foot had remained numb. Luckily there was an excellent osteopath in Perth, and after treatment his foot was restored to normal circulation.

Hard as we tried to get passages, we were told each time that whilst Charles could go, I should have to wait to return with Jane. We refused to be parted, and at last all three of us were granted passages on a converted Lancaster, which was leaving for England on 15 December.

The remaining time we spent in Perth·was completely hectic for there were so many people we had to see, and we wanted to thank all those who had been so kind to Jane.

Each morning, when possible, I took charge of Ferne, and had her down by the River Swan, where we soon renewed our old friendship. Her mother was slowly improving in health, though it was to be some months before she was able to make the journey to England by boat.

By 12 December we were in a steady whirl of entertainment and shopping, as we'd received letters to warn of shortages of food, soap and clothing at home. We dared not take much, since we might not be allowed on the plane. As it was, at the last moment we were off-loaded for Christmas mail. Fortunately Charles got busy, and once more we were told to be ready at 4.30 A.M. Jane, who hadn't previously flown, was wondering whether she liked the idea or not, and with all the excitement and the great sadness at leaving our dear friends the Millers, as well as school friends, she did not know if she was on her head or her heels.

It was a sad moment when we said goodbye to the Millers, who came to the airport, and would have been much sadder had I known that Nell was to die six months later. She was a wonderful woman, and none of us will ever forget her. Later Titus came back to England, and lived with us in Cornwall.

From Perth we flew to Learmouth, stopping on the way to pick up passengers from lonely out-stations.

Everyone with whom we came in contact in the RAAF station in Learmouth seemed surprised to find a woman and a girl amongst the passengers, but a kindly crew member cleared out of his hut for us. Sand was everywhere, and when the men were bathing in the nearby sea, sharks paraded about thirty yards from the shore, their fins sticking out of the water.

We had to wait for our plane to arrive from Sydney, and I suddenly got a terrible presentiment that we should come down in the sea if we took off. I didn't dare say a word, as we had had so much trouble to get passages together, and was still frightened when the Sydney plane, a converted Lancaster, arrived. Fortunately, after some delay, we were told there was a cyclone in the Indian Ocean and we would have to stay the night.

As we fastened our seat belts the next day, and felt the thrust of the engines, we realized that we were really on the last lap of our journey to England and the family.

27

Home for Christmas

Flying through the night on the longest, fastest hop, we landed about 9.30 A.M. at Ngombo Airport in Ceylon where, together with the other passengers, an Air Commodore and a Lloyds man, we had breakfast. About 10.30 we left again, and flew all day over India, arriving at Karachi at about 6 P.M. We stayed a few hours for refuelling, and had supper at the airport.

Jane, having stood the journey very well, was feeling the change from heat to cold and back to heat each time we landed, and spent much of the time in a rug, sleeping. Having reached Karachi after only twenty-four hours' flying, we felt there was a good chance we should soon be home, and as we looked down on the lighted flares as we flew over the aerodrome, we wondered if we would really be in England the following evening.

Alas for our hopes! When we got to Lydda at 4 A.M., we heard the weather over Europe was so bad we were to be diverted to Tripoli, and would have to wait for better flying conditions there. In fact, we got to Castel Benito airport in time to go by bus to Tripoli, where we had a second breakfast.

Much as we wanted to get home, the enforced rest in a comfortable hotel mainly occupied still by British officers and officials at that time did us good.

When we arrived at the hotel, we were told it was impossible to say how long we would have to wait there, as planes had already been grounded for some days – there were heavy snowstorms at the time all over Europe – but that we should be taken on as soon as possible.

When we went to the dining room, which was reached by a passage constructed under the main road, we found it was built out by the sea, and Jane was delighted to find that we even had spaghetti for breakfast. Our efforts to cope with it caused much amusement amongst the Italian waiters.

That evening, the third since leaving Australia, we were warned there was a chance that the weather just might clear up sufficiently for us to be able to fly on, and the following morning at seven we were once more motoring back through the flat fields and olive groves to the airport, which lay some way outside the town.

At last we were to make the final lap of our long journey home, which had taken us from Java to Singapore, Singapore to Western Australia, and finally, from Australia across three continents, home, and we could hardly believe it was happening.

We took off, and flew over Sardinia, and then over France, where the mountains were covered with snow, and storms raged above and below us. At three o'clock in the afternoon we landed without mishap at Hurn Airport. We were home for Christmas!

Everything was arranged most efficiently, and after being passed by the doctor and the various authorities, we went through Customs, where our small amount of luggage was quickly passed. We had been very lucky to have so smooth a flight, for very shortly after our arrival the West African plane landed, and all the passengers looked absolutely green after the terrible trip they'd had.

Standing beside us in the Customs was a man from the African plane, and, as we watched, a dark brown liquid came slowly out of his case, across the table, and went drip! drip! on to the ground. Heads were lifted and noses sniffed the air, and several of the passengers looked as if they wished they had had a glass handy. The poor man had broken one of his precious bottles of brandy he was bringing home as a Christmas gift.

All the London passengers were taken by bus to Bournemouth to catch their train. As it steamed into the station in London, we hopefully scanned the enormous crowd, looking for any of the family. Daphne was not there, though my sister was, as it had been thought best for Daphne to return to her aunt when our plane was delayed, and we did not actually see her until the following evening.

By the greatest bad luck the telegram giving the time of her arrival at Victoria Station did not reach us until much later, and so she not only had to make her way alone from the station to our hotel, but was not at all sure that after eight years she would recognize us when she did see us.

Luckily the three of us were sitting near the door, still hoping we would hear from her, when it suddenly opened and she came in.

At first we were all rather shy, but then Daphne and Jane went off together to their room, and when we went to collect them for dinner they were hard at it, chattering as hard as they could go. Before very long we were once more the happy, loving family we had been before the war.

Epilogue

Now that many years have passed, during which my husband and I had a son, Simon, to the delight of us all, and we settled back in Cornwall, I can look with a kinder eye on the years of internment, and my return to Java in 1948.

When we reached England at the end of 1945, we had no home, possessions or money. Because Charles had worked in a foreign country, in compensation for all of our losses we received from the Government only £36 each, with a further bonus of £8 each for Christmas. We were not allowed to take over our little farm, for which the sitting tenants still only paid £19 per year. We therefore cashed our insurance, which did not cover wars, to buy a small bungalow beside the farm.

We had only been able to bring minimal luggage from Australia for fear of being off-loaded, but when my husband honestly told the local authorities that he hoped if possible to return to Java one day, he was told he could not have coupons for clothes, blankets, sheets, etc. Until there was a chance to get back to the estates, the Company itself could only hand out limited money to staff, and we found it extremely hard to manage.

In August, 1947, Charles was able to return to West Java with a small group of British and Dutch staff, to restart the plantation company, the fourth largest in the world.

Conditions were primitive, and many of the buildings had been bombed and destroyed after the Japanese occupation, during the fighting between Dutch troops and Indonesians.

Parts of West and East Java were then held by the Dutch, and a force was stationed in Soebang. In March, 1948, I was able to fly out via Singapore, and the other Dutch wives came down from Bandoeng to join their husbands. It had been too dangerous for me to take Simon with me, and the first night I arrived back with my husband, a bullet flew through our bedroom shutter.

I was extremely worried over Charles's health since the arduous and dangerous conditions, added to all the worry of restarting the Company, getting necessary finance and permits, and deaths of members of our staff as well as of the Army, had left him thin and suffering from occasional blackouts. In fact, we attended funerals of soldiers killed in fighting, or staff who had been murdered, nearly every week.

When I flew out, I had hoped to persuade Charles to return to England with me, but he loved the place and the people, and felt he must do all he could to help resettle many of the Dutch families who had been through such terrible years, and give the thousands of estate workers a chance of a more settled life.

He was later to receive the decoration of the Oranje Nassau from the Dutch Government, as well as a letter of thanks from the RAF for all the help he had given, but no award could really hope to repay his constant thought for others, both during internment and after the war.

In the end, we did not leave Java until March, 1949,

when I persuaded Charles he had done more than enough for the Company, and should return home.

Fighting continued between the Dutch and the Indonesians on a bitter and deadly scale, despite the efforts to effect a reconciliation. Finally, independence was attained on 23 August 1949, at the Hague Conference, and Dr Soekarno became the first President.

In 1950 we moved to London, where Charles became managing director, and later chairman of the Company. During the ensuing years my husband paid many visits to Java, and on seven occasions I accompanied him to give what help I could. All estates by then had Indonesian managers, and I was able to meet the wives, which I much enjoyed, and talk to groups of Indonesian women.

I made many friends, and it was a great sadness when the British, too, had to leave Indonesia, and I could no longer keep in touch with friends in that beautiful island.

In 1962 we retired to Cornwall for thirteen happy years. Charles died, aged eighty-two, after we had had, despite much sadness, a wonderful forty-five years of marriage.